IMAGES OF THE GRAND TOUR

Louis Ducros 1748–1810

**This exhibition has been organized by the GLC
and the Musée cantonal des Beaux-Arts, Lausanne**
with generous support from
**Fondation Pro Helvetia, Zürich
Commission cantonale des Activités Culturelles du Canton de Vaud
The Swiss Banks registered in Great Britain
The Visiting Arts Unit of Great Britain
Greater Manchester Council**

**EDITIONS du TRICORNE
GENEVA**

fig. 1   P-L de la Rive, *Portrait of Ducros as a Young Man*, Lausanne (MCBA).

IMAGES OF THE GRAND TOUR
Louis Ducros 1748–1810

THE IVEAGH BEQUEST, KENWOOD
Hampstead Lane, London NW3 7JR

4 September—31 October 1985

Open daily: 10–7 September, 10–5 October
Greater London Council

THE WHITWORTH ART GALLERY
University of Manchester
Oxford Road, Manchester M15 6ER

10 January—22 February 1986

Open daily: 10–5, Thursday 10–9,
closed Sunday
Supported by
Greater Manchester Council

MUSEE CANTONAL DES
BEAUX-ARTS
Place de la Riponne, CH 1005 Lausanne
21 March—19 May 1986

Abbreviations

MCBA	Musée cantonal des Beaux-Arts, Lausanne
ACV	Archives cantonales vaudoises, Lausanne
BPU	Bibliothèque publique et universitaire (manuscripts), Geneva
BCU	Bibliothèque cantonale et universitaire (manuscripts), Lausanne
ACY	Archives communales, Yverdon
AV	Archivio del Vicariato, Rome
BM	The British Museum
s&d	signed and dated
l.	left
r.	right
t.	top
b.	bottom

Text set in Monotype Times and printed by
BAS Printers Limited, Over Wallop, Hampshire.

Colour illustrations printed by
Imprimerie Bron sa Lausanne, Switzerland

ISBN 2-8293-0060-2

COVER: Louis Ducros *The Arch of Titus*
(Catalogue No. 1.)

CONTENTS

FOREWORD

Ducros may not be a household name today, but in the late eighteenth and early nineteenth centuries this Swiss artist was regarded by artists and collectors as one of the most important figures in the development of landscape painting in water-colours. He appealed particularly to those who had made the Grand Tour to Rome and Naples, providing English houses with definitive images of the Grand Tour with an emphatic European professionalism. One of his major patrons, Sir Richard Colt Hoare of Stourhead, writing in 1822, even claimed his work to be the essential link between the drawings of Paul Sandby and the paintings of J M W Turner, stating that 'the advancement from *drawing* to *painting* in water-colours did not take place till after the introduction into England of the drawings of Louis du Cros'.

Ducros certainly took water-colour beyond its traditional limits: he strengthened his drawings—on an unusually large scale—with body-colour or *gouache*, oil and varnish. The several pieces of paper required were often joined together and pasted onto canvas, before framing under glass. He produced water-colours suitable for hanging to decorative effect as pictures, rather than drawings destined to the confines of portfolios and collectors' cabinets. He gave his water-colours a brilliance and depth which would vie with oil paintings, anticipating the 'exhibition' water-colours of the nineteenth century. He achieved a grander vision of Rome—or Naples or Malta—with deceptions of scale, exaggerated proportions of ancient monuments, condensing the landscape through a variety of artistic devices, including wide-angle vision and multiple viewpoints, which recall the majestic engravings of his older Roman contemporary, G. B. Piranesi. Ducros was not above using the techniques of engraving himself, producing outline etchings that could be hand coloured to satisfy the souvenir market in Italy, 'water-colours' which have since been frequently mistaken for originals. Inevitably his reputation has suffered, and modern opinion has become largely equivocal: the first exhibitions were held in Lausanne over thirty years ago, but now with the benefit of modern scholarship, and an international selection of loans it is possible to re-assess the substance of Colt Hoare's claim. It is hoped that this exhibition will establish Ducros once again as one of the major figures in the development of water-colour painting.

The staff of The Iveagh Bequest and of The Whitworth Art Gallery are indebted to Pierre Chessex of the Musée Historique de l'Ancien Evêché, Lausanne, who not only initiated this exhibition, but whose research on Ducros forms the basis of the catalogue. M Chessex has selected the European loans, as well as those from the Ducros Collection in Lausanne, and written the individual entries for the catalogue. The British loans have been selected by Miss Lindsay Stainton of the Department of Prints and Drawings of the British Museum, who has not only written the entries but also contributed an essay on the importance of Ducros to British artists and collectors. In the selection she has been assisted by Julius Bryant, Assistant Curator at Kenwood, who has also arranged for the translation of the catalogue and has been responsible for seeing the English edition through the press. We are also grateful to Professor Francis Haskell, Luc Boissonnas, Westby Percival Prescott and Olivier Masson for providing essays on the artistic context and techniques of Ducros' work.

No exhibition on this scale is possible without the generous support of many lenders, both public and private, and the willing co-operation of the staff of the institutions involved. Particular thanks are due to the National Trust, to the Bayerische Staatsbibliothek, Munich, the Goethe-Museum, Frankfurt, the Museo di Roma, the Rijksmuseum, Amsterdam and the Pavlovsk Palace Museum, USSR. The exhibition has been generously supported by the Fondation Pro Helvetia, Swiss Banks in this country and by a grant towards the cost of the English language catalogue by the Visiting Arts Unit of Great Britain. To all these individuals and institutions we are profoundly grateful.

Finally, we should like to record our gratitude—in this year of all years—to the GLC and the Greater Manchester Council for their continual support, which has enabled international exhibitions such as this to become a regular feature of the exhibition calendar. For Kenwood the exhibition marks the continuation of a series of exhibitions on the theme of British patrons and the Grand Tour in the eighteenth century, while for the Whitworth it complements one of the major collections of water-colours in the North of England—a collection which also includes two of the few works by Ducros in public, as opposed to private ownership, in this country.

John Jacob
Curator, GLC Historic Houses
The Iveagh Bequest, Kenwood

ACKNOWLEDGEMENTS

The importance of the Swiss painter Abraham-Louis-Rodolphe Ducros to the history of the landscape water-colour was recognised even in the writings of his contemporaries, notably Bridel (1790), Meusel (1797), Schlegel and Goethe (1805) and Guattani (1807). In England Sir Richard Colt Hoare was the first to appreciate the painter's qualities in *The History of Modern Wiltshire* (1822). William T Whitley took up the case for Ducros again in 1928 and intelligent contributions were to follow from C F Bell and Tom Girtin in 1934–35. Modern historians have been prepared to accord Ducros a place of honour (Martin Hardie, 1975, 3rd edition; Luke Herrmann, 1973) but have not had the necessary material to hand to make a true evaluation of his importance. Until today we have not been sufficiently familiar with his works, nor have we been sure of their dates. The aim of this exhibition is to give the British public the opportunity to see Ducros' Italian landscapes, the majority of which are in Switzerland at the Musée cantonal des Beaux-Arts, Lausanne.

This exhibition is not a celebration of Ducros, for the paintings have been chosen primarily for their documentary interest. Neither is it a definitive survey of the painter's work, as there are still too many grey areas. It is really a starting point: knowledge of the work of this artist should provide a basis for wider debate on the role he played between 1780 and 1810, when the landscape as an independent genre was taking on greater importance. The quality of his water-colours, the complexity of his methods and the imposing scale of his landscapes are all elements which should contribute to the re-examination of his position among foreign artists in Italy in the late eighteenth century.

This exhibition could not have been mounted without the support of the Greater London Council, the Greater Manchester Council, the Fondation Pro Helvetia and the Vaud canton. But it is above all to the enthusiasm and expertise of John Jacob, Julius Bryant and all the staff at Kenwood that I owe this opportunity of presenting the works of Ducros in Great Britain today. Let me not forget Michael Clarke, who from the very beginning supported me in the idea of mounting an exhibition in England.

I would also like to thank the following people and institutions for their help:

Robert and Odette Achard, Luisa Arrigoni, Joanna Banham, Yvonne Boerlin-Brodbeck, Frances Berendt, Jacques-Edouard Berger, Carlo Bertelli, Erika Billeter, Luc Boissonnas, Helmut Börsch-Supan, Giuliano Briganti, Iain G Brown, Jean-Daniel Candaux, Enrico Castelnuovo, Lucia Cavazzi, Christiane Chessex-Viguet, André Coigny, Belinda Cousens, Karl Dachs, Florens Deuchler, Patrick Devanthéry, Gemma Di Domenico Cortese, Stella Dyer, Christoph Eggenberger, Fonds National de la Recherche Scientifique (Berne), Eraldo Gaudioso, Georg Germann, Mary Goodwin, St. John Gore, Marcel Grandjean, Pontus Grate, Marianne von Grueningen, Francis Haskell, William Hauptman, Francis Hawcroft, J P Haworth, Anne de Herdt, Franziska Heuss, Uwe Hinkfoth, Ragnar von Holten, Jean Hugli, Sarah Hyde, Istituto Svizzero di Roma (Clemens Krause, dir.), Marie-Claude Jéquier, Philippe Junod, Sandor Küthy, Christina Kröll, Johannes Kunz, Inès Lamunière, Michel Liebman, Milan Lusser, Hans A Lüthy, Petra Maisak, Sylvain Malfroy, Renzo Mancini, Ernest Manganel, Laura Mascoli, Olivier Masson, Flavio Meroni, Olivier Michel, Anthony Mitchell, Bernard and François Naef, Mauro Natale, J W Niemeijer, Werner Oechslin, Christoph Perels, Francois Pictet, Jean-Yves Pidoux, Carlo Pietrangeli, W Percival Prescott, Hubert Prouté, Casimir de Rham, Claude Reymond, Emiliana Ricci, Giovanni Romano, Y Roussakov, Francis Russell, Frieder Ryser, Pierre Sabatier, Birgitta Sandstroem, R W Scheller, M and Mme Claude Secretan, Société Académique Vaudoise, Société Vaudoise des Beaux-Arts, Mme Stadnitchouk, Lindsay Stainton, Mary Ann Stevens, Teresa Sulerzyska, Julian Tomlin, Georges Vallet, Anne and Udolpho Van de Sandt, Mario Verdone, Elena Vuille-Mondada, Laurette Wettstein, Stephen Wildman, Kenneth Woodbridge, Lucas Wüthrich, Bernard Wyder, Padre M J Zerafa.

P C

CHRONOLOGY

1748

21st July: Abraham-Louis-Rodolphe Ducros born in Moudon, Vaud, Switzerland, the son of Jean-Rodolphe, a writing and drawing master.

1750

The Ducros family live in Yverdon. Two more sons born: in 1750, Louis-Guillaume-Samuel, who followed in his father's footsteps and spent his whole career in Yverdon, and in 1751, Francois-Barthélemy, who became a minister.

1761

Jean-Rodolphe Ducros purchases citizenship of Yverdon.

1764

16th June: Death of Jean-Rodolphe. His widow allows the sons to inherit, in spite of their youth. Abraham-Louis-Rodolphe takes over his father's post at the college.

1765

13th April: 'The two Ducros brothers, both schoolmasters, having presented examples of drawing and handwriting, are favourably accorded thirty florins from the town' (ACY, Council Register). 'The elder Master Ducros, son of the late Master Ducros, who had jointly with his brother been entrusted with the charge of the third class, wishing to remove elsewhere for his greater advantage, has been permitted to do so by the Council' (Ibid.).

1768–70

According to Bridel, Ducros makes a start in commerce, but 'he was a born painter; he could only be a painter; at first he stole moments from his everyday occupations in order to draw; soon he grew to dislike commerce, left his desk and Geneva, and travelled across Italy to arrive at the holy place of art' (*Etrennes Helvétiennes*, 1790). In fact, from 1769 he studied at the private academy of the Chevalier de Fassin (Nicolas-H-Joseph Fassin, 1728–1811) in Geneva, and copied the work of many Flemish and Dutch masters.

1771–72

Ducros travels with his master in Flanders, but 'left him and in Geneva found friends and all the help he needed' (*Journal de Genève*, 1789).

1773–76

In Geneva he copies Wouwerman, Berchem, J Both and Ruysdael. According to his companion, the young painter Pierre-Louis de la Rive (1753–1817), he also painted many water-colours of the countryside around Geneva and in Savoy (De la Rive, 1832).

1775

Gian Angelo Braschi elected Pope Pius VI. Artists arriving in Rome include J L David (who stays until 1779), Jacques Sablet, J M Vien and William Pars.

1776

Richard Cooper, John Robert Cozens, Thomas Jones, John 'Warwick' Smith and, at the end of the year, Bénigne Gagneraux and the Swiss sculptor Alexandre Trippel, all arrive in Rome. In the summer 'Ducros, tired of copying, decided at this time to go to Rome' (De la Rive, 1832). He travels with Isaac-Jacob La Croix, an engraver formerly in the Basle workshop of the famous Christian von Mechel (Fuesslin, 1779). They make the usual stops in Bologna and Florence and arrive in Rome at the end of the year.

1777

Pierre-Henri de Valenciennes arrives in Rome and remains until 1782. Ducros lodges in the Campo Marzo quarter comprising the parishes of San Lorenzo in Lucina, Santa Maria del Popolo and Sant' Andrea delle Fratte, near the Spanish Steps. His name can be found in the registers of the parish of San Lorenzo for almost every year until 1793.

1778

Death of Piranesi. Fuseli leaves Rome for London, travelling via Zurich. Ducros lodges with his compatriot La Croix at the home of the painter Fortunato Vercelli in the Strada delle Carrozze (AV, S Lorenzo, Liber status animarum, 1778, fol 45/v.)
March–April: Ducros engaged by the Dutchman Nicolas Ten Hove to accompany him and two gentlemen from The Hague, W C Dierkens and W H van Nieuwerkerke, on a trip to the Kingdom of the Two Sicilies.
10th April: Departure for Naples via Terracina and Gaeta.
12th April: Arrival in Naples. Visit to Sir William Hamilton.
18th April: Departure for the South. Avellino, Paterno, Canosa di Puglia, Barletta, Trani.
25th April: Day spent resting in Bari. 'The painter accompanying us, most skilled and with an untiring enthusiasm for his art, left early in the morning to paint some views of the town' (Nieuwerkerke's manuscript journal; extract kindly provided by Dr J W Niemeijer).
End of April: Their coaches get stuck in the mud arriving at Brindisi, a misadventure related by Dominique Vivant-Denon who got stuck at the same time as Ducros and his companions (Saint-Non, *Voyage pittoresque*, vol III, chap 3, p 52). Lecce. Gallipoli.
3rd May: Casalnuovo, visit to the ruins of ancient Mandusia: 'Ten Hove had several drawings made, which are all the more unusual in that the temples are little-known' (Ibid.).

Taranto, then by boat to Reggio di Calabria and then on to Messina.

14th–19th May: Messina. Meeting with the Genevan merchant Brechthel, then by boat to Scilla.

20th May: With a fleet of *speronari* (small boats) to Taormina.

28th–30th May: Catania. Etna.

1st–5th June: Syracuse.

6th–7th June: With the *speronari* to Malta.

8th–16th June: Malta. Gozo.

17th–25th June: Crossing on a French boat from Valletta to Agrigento.

25th–28th June: Agrigento: 'At Girgenti the most beautiful antiquities in Sicily are to be found . . . Ten Hove studied them and had drawings made'. (Dierkens' manuscript journal, Rijksprentenkabinet, Amsterdam).

29th June–15th July: Palermo. Excursion to Segesta. Feast of Santa Rosalia.

16th–20th July: Crossing from Palermo to Naples on a French brigantine.

26th July: Climbed Vesuvius.

28th–29th July: Dining at the villa of Sir William and Lady Hamilton in Posillipo.

12th August: Return to Rome: 'After dinner we saw Monsieur Ducros' drawings which are very beautiful, and also beautiful paintings by a French artist named Thiers'. (Ibid.).

Surviving works: Dessins/de mon voyage dans les Deux Siciles/et/à Malte/1778/Louis Ducros fecit. (see cat no 51–53); *A view of the harbour at Pozzuoli near Naples,* water-colour, s.d. 1778 (see cat no 63).

1779

La Croix returns to Switzerland after working as an engraver for Giovanni Volpato and J P Hackert (fig 6); at the end of the year he engraves plates for Charles Bonnet's *Mémoire sur la Reproduction des membres de la Salamandre aquatique* in Geneva. Ducros begins his collaboration with Volpato.

Surviving work: Temple of Peace, water-colour, s.d., Yale Center for British Art, New Haven.

1780

Francis Towne arrives in Rome.
Ducros living on the Via del Corso (AV, S Lorenzo, 1780, fol 66/v). Publishes the first twenty-four of his *Vues de Rome et de ses environs* in association with Giovanni Volpato. Raffaele Morghen etches a seascape after Ducros (according to Palmerini, 1824, pp 10–11).

Surviving work: Roman landscape, oil, s.d., Kunstmuseum, Bern.

1781

Ducros lives at the same address in the Via del Corso (AV, S Lorenzo, 1781, fol 65). Peter Birman (1758–1844) engaged as an assistant. Birman, who had worked with J L Aberli in Bern, starts drawing for Ducros but the two argue over financial matters and he leaves for Volpato's workshop.

'M Desprez has settled in Rome and taken up with [F] Piranesi: they have undertaken a series of drawings which have deservedly earned the greatest success. . . . Ducroc is still here. He has taken up with Volpato and they are publishing coloured views of Rome. The novelty should have helped them to sell, but the work of Messieurs Desprez and Piranesi is capturing all the attention and Ducroc has not a single

advocate. Sablé is back from Switzerland—he is in uniform' (Letter from Masreliez to Wertmüller, 26th September 1781, Stockholm, Royal Library, Ep. V 12:4 fol 9). 'M Ducros of Yverdon, who has gained an excellent reputation in Rome, is working, in collaboration with M Volpato on a collection of illuminated views of Rome; twelve pieces in the format of the *School of Athens* are finished, as are twelve of medium size.' (Meusel, 1781).

1782

Ducros now in the Strada della Croce, his accommodation serving as both studio and showroom. There he sells his own work, the coloured engravings made with Volpato, Sablet and Morghen, and some by other artists such as Desprez and F Piranesi. During this year Sablet shares his accommodation (AV, S Lorenzo, 1782–83, fol. 27).

Ducros makes a series of twelve wash engravings of Italian costumes after drawings by Sablet (see Sablet catalogue, 1985, nos 76–87). *A Funeral before the Pyramid of Cestius,* made by the same method but in a different format, could be from a slightly later date.

Surviving works: Ducros with Dr Tissot and Marc Dapples in the Baths of Caracalla, formerly collection of Madame de Stietencron, Château de Crissier, Switzerland, currently unlocated (reproduced in Sévery, 1911, II, p 192). *The Grand Duke Paul and the Grand Duchess Maria at Tivoli* and *The Grand Duke Paul in the Forum,* two large oils painted during Grand Duke Paul Romanov's trip to Italy in February and March (now in Pavlovsk Palace, Leningrad, see cat no 56). Ducros' fame reached his homeland. An almanack of 1783 mentions him in Rome, where 'he has published coloured engravings of different views of this capital; he reproduces ancient ruins with a particularly striking veracity' (*Etrennes Helvétiennes,* 1783).

1783

Jacques Sablet now living in the Casa al Mosaico, Via Margutta, with the Genevan painter Jean-Pierre Saint-Ours and some other Protestant artists (AV, S Maria del Popolo, 1783, fol 46).

March–April: Ducros accompanies Pope Pius VI to the Pontine marshes (see cat no 55); a letter he wrote to Charles Bonnet indicates that he was favoured by the pontiff: 'His Holiness has shown me the greatest favour in the audiences he has accorded me, and, as I was retiring after the first visit he called me back and invited me with the greatest kindness to dine at liberty at his first table with his prelates and courtiers during his stay in Terracina. I laughed to myself at the thought of a child of Calvin, a heretic, sitting in the shadow of the banners of the Church, eating ambrosia and drinking nectar destined for the Saints. . . . I have found the courtiers to be nothing but machines, pulled only by the strings of self-interest. Ah! How I prefer to be beneath the cascades of Tivoli at sunrise where Newton could split light without a prism. . . .' (BPU, 7th July 1783, MS. Bonnet, 37). The painter stayed regularly in Tivoli, and in the Sabine hills and Umbria. Weinbrunner tells of a peasant he met in Papigno near Terni, who remembered Ducros' travels in the region and proudly said that the painter even became godfather of one of his children (Weinbrunner, 1958, p 110). Lord Breadalbane is said to have acquired works by Ducros (Ford, 1974, p 450). 'Went from there [i.e. Porta Pia] to Mr De Cro who shewd us [the party may have included Jacob More, in whose company Ramsay had already been that day] some of his works which were very pretty but particularly those in Aqua [?acquarello] which surpass any thing I ever saw of it. Went at 3 to Ld. Bredalbane's where we found Mr Byres and Mr Hamilton. Ld. Bredalbane shewd us two drawings he had got of De Cro's the one of the Pantheon and the other of Antoninus and Faustina's portico, which were exceedingly well done.' *John Ramsay's Italian Journal* 29th March 1783, pp 56–7, National Library of Scotland MS 1833, reference kindly provided by Dr Iain G Brown. *Surviving work: Pius VI visiting the drainage works at the Pontine Marshes*, oil, Pavlovsk (see cat no 55).

1784

Pierre-Louis de la Rive arrives in Rome and stays until the beginning of 1786. His correspondence with his wife provides an interesting source for the study of artistic circles in the period (Morsier, 1972). Ducros still resident in the Strada della Croce (AV, S Lorenzo, 1784–85, fol 32/v). The King of Sweden, Gustav III, visits Ducros in his studio at the end of the former's stay in Rome, as related in the *Diario Ordinario*, no 972, 24th April 1784: 'The famous painter M Ducros was honoured with a visit from His Majesty the King of Sweden, and dedicated to His Majesty two engravings in the manner of a wash drawing, one representing a sacrifice to Venus, the other a sacrifice to Eros; the sovereign . . . presented him personally with a superb medal in gold showing his portrait on one side, and on the other a trophy of the fine arts'. It seems that Ducros was approached to become Commissioner for Antiquities to the Court of Sweden, but Francesco Piranesi, who had a greater reputation, was finally chosen (Wollin, 1933, p 32). Gustav III was passionately interested in antiquity and had visited Volpato several times. Since 1779, in addition to running his engraving studio, Volpato had been undertaking archaeological excavations authorised by Pius VI at Frascati, the Baths of Caracalla and other sites. It was probably on these visits by Gustav that the numerous views by Ducros and Volpato were acquired. They are today shared between the castle of Drottningholm, the Royal Palace and the Nationalmuseum in Stockholm.
Surviving works: Pio VI Max. Emisarium Paludis Pontinae Desperatum Opus Excogitavit. Mediterraneo Perduxit. Suo nomine illustravit.— Ed Antonio Casalio Cardinali, Turris Gregoriana Prope Terracinam. These two hand coloured engravings signed: *Romae ANNO MDCCLXXXIV, L. R. Du Cros Helveticus DDD.* Two engravings given to Gustav III by Ducros, Royal Palace, Stockholm.
Vue d'Ariccia, water-colour, currently unlocated, formerly William Spooner collection, (see cat no 29).

1785

Frederick Hervey, Bishop of Derry and 4th Earl of Bristol commissions from Ducros *Cicero discovering the tomb of Archimedes at Syracuse* (currently unlocated). The painting was in hand at the end of 1784 when Ducros was visited by his compatriot August Pidou, guide and private tutor to Lord Downe on the Grand Tour (Vulliemin, 1860).
Ducros paints the cascades of Terni and Tivoli for Lord Breadalbane. Lord Grey, later 1st Earl of Wilton, noted the following in his *Journal of my Tour on the Continent in the years 1784 and 1785*: 'We went to see the paintings of M du Cros, a landscape painter who seems to have a good deal of merit. His views of the Fall of Terni are much admired. We next proceeded to the house of Pompeo Batoni' (16th March 1785, diary owned by Lord Wilton, on loan to Manchester City Art Gallery. fol 81–82, reference kindly provided by Michael Clarke). The *Memorie per le Belle Arti* of April 1785 refers to all these commissions with great praise for Ducros' landscapes. The same Roman journal mentions Gustav III's commissions for Sablet, Jacob More's landscapes for Lord Breadalbane, the bust of Cardinal Albani by Trippel and finally J L David's *Oath of the Horatii*. Four hand-coloured outline etchings by Ducros and Volpato bought by James Byres on behalf of William Constable: *Villa Borghese, Temple of Peace, Tivoli* and *Civitavecchia* (Ford, 1974, pp 414–415). Thirty-four hand-coloured outline etchings (eighteen large ones, eight medium-sized and eight small) purchased by Baron Carl Sparre, the Swedish senator who accompanied Gustav III on his Italian journey. Francesco Piranesi acted as intermediary, according to a letter from Ducros to Sparre of 18th Novermber 1785, where he discusses the purchase and uses the opportunity to request patronage: 'Your Excellency, who is so powerful at the Court, grant me the favour of not forgetting completely the Haga article, and, as with Cavalier Sergell, propose me to His Majesty so that I may have the honour of having some of my paintings in Stockholm'. (Stockholm, Rijkarchivet, E 3051).
Ducros sends a picture from his years in Geneva to his patron, the naturalist Charles Bonnet who thanks him in a letter of 20th August 1785. This letter also reveals that Catherine the Great had bought works by Ducros: 'Your fine picture, which reached us in an excellent state, has been admired by all the connoisseurs and it is one of the principal decorations in our drawing room . . ., I still have to congratulate you on the repeated marks of esteem you have received from the Pontiff: they would lead me to presume that he knows the value of the fine arts and how they may become representative of a reign. The Semiramis of the North knows this too, and your honourable brother has given us great pleasure in telling us that your work has reached her' (BPU, MS Bonnet 76).
Bonnet's letter reached Ducros at Tivoli where 'I was as usual paying court to Nature in her beauty in this region which is so full of picturesque sites' (21st October 1785, MS Bonnet 38).

1786

Ducros still resident at the same address (AV, S Lorenzo, 1786, fol 32). The painter meets Richard Colt Hoare who was to become a great admirer of his work and his most important client. Colt Hoare buys four large water-colours: *Lake Trasimeno, View at Tivoli* (cat no 68), *Ponte Lucano* and *Città Castellana* (now at Stourhead, Wiltshire). From 1787 to 1791 he commissions another eight large pictures and two hand-coloured outline etchings

(see cat nos 69–73). According to Woodbridge (1970, p 97), Colt Hoare corresponded with the painter, and one letter survives (see Appendix 1). Sir Richard also took notes on Ducros' water-colour technique and records that he 'shewd me a very easy method of engraving drawings in the brown tints' (cit. Woodbridge, 1970, p 96). According to J G Meusel's *Miscellaneen* (1786, p 246) Ducros was preparing a treatise on making etchings with a brush and quill but this work is untraced. Several engravings produced by this technique are known: two of Terracina dedicated to Pius VI and Cardinal Casali in 1784, two given to Gustav III, and the series of scenes from Italian life after drawings by Sablet.
Surviving works: Pius VI visiting the drainage works at the Pontine Marshes s.d., Museo di Roma (see cat no 55); *Marble Cascade, Terni* (distant view), Rome art market, 1983 (reproduced as *Cascade à Tivoli* in exhibition catalogue, Rome, 1980, p 84) (see cat no 25).

1787

Still resident in the Strada della Croce (AV, S Lorenzo. 1787, fol. 32), Ducros is mentioned in the list of painters living in Rome in 1787 made by Alois Hirt: 'du Cros of Lausanne, in his fortieth year, has the great merit of painting drawings with water-colour after nature. The veracity of his cascades, the brilliance of his ruins and a certain vaporous transparency in all his landscapes could not be brought to a higher level in this genre, and the same may be said of his prices which reach 25 to 30 gold louis. He has been doing a great deal of business for several years'. (Quoted in Eckhardt, 1979). Hendrik Fagel, a Dutch traveller, gained the same impression on 6th January, 1787: 'Of the landscape artists few enjoy such a reputation as Ducros, a Swiss by birth, the same who undertook the journey in Sicily with cousin Ten Hove and uncle Dierkens, and whose drawings are in the possession of cousin Ten Hove. This painter now has so much to do that he sells a single water-colour for 300 to 350 florins. It may be true that there is nothing finer or more perfect to be found, but that is still a lot for a painting' (The Hague, State Archives, Arch. Fagel no 2661; text kindly provided by Dr J W Niemeijer).
Philippe Secretan, another Swiss, noted in his diary on 3rd January: 'On leaving my inn I went to Ducros'—he was surrounded by pictures. Two Englishmen were showering him with praise; I was expecting to meet a compatriot, but I found only a cold producer of landscapes engaged in selling gouaches to the English' (BCU, Fonds PELIS Is 4350, fol 32). Several days later Secretan returned to Ducros' studio and this time found in him 'an honest, cordial and obliging fellow. I quite saw my compatriot in him. He showed me a very fine gouache of the Temple of the Sibyl', (Ibid. fol 61). In *Museum für Künstler* (1787) Meusel praises the series of eight etched views coloured by Ducros and engraved around 1785 by Raffaele Morghen (see cat no 29).
Ducros is mentioned for the first time in a directory: 'Ducros and Vopato; these two artists are publishing in Rome coloured views of different forms and sizes; *View of the Temple of Minerva*, in colour.' (Huber, 1787, p 42).

1788–89

Ducros still in his studio in the Strada della

Croce, according to the census taken at Easter AV, S Lorenzo, 1788, fol 26/v). In collaboration with Volpato he publishes fourteen coloured views of the new rooms in the Museo Pio-Clementino (see cat no 57–62). In 1786 Volpato opened a factory for biscuit porcelain statuettes which reproduced the most famous classical statues, some of which were exhibited in the Vatican. The publication was to be Ducros' last collaboration with Volpato, and he now arranged with the Roman publisher Pier Paolo Montagnani to produce a series of twenty-four views of Sicily and Malta. In July 1789 Bridel describes him as 'at present working on a Sicilian project, containing twenty-four views of that famous island' (*Etrennes Helvétiennes*, 1790). Ducros probably travels south in the winter of 1788–89, as Bridel's report suggest.
At the first Salon de la Société des Arts in Geneva Ducros exhibits *View of Paestum* and *Temple of Concord (Agrigento)*, along with *Cascades at Terni* (nos 27, 29 and 37 respectively in the *Notice des tableaux*, 1789).
The series of engravings announced for publication by Ducros and Montagnani never seem to have been published in their entirety. Tischbein's note relating the visit by Ducros and Gagneraux to his Neapolitan academy probably dates from this time (Tischbein, 1861).

1790–91

The repercussions of the French Revolution begin to be felt in Rome. Artists receive fewer commissions, but Ducros agrees to take on a compatriot as his assistant, the young painter François Kaiserman (1765–1833) who is recorded as sharing his accommodation in the Strada della Croce (AV, S Lorenzo, 1790–91, fol 32/v). The Republican ideal spreads to Rome, and Pius VI takes 'preventive measures', ordering surveillance of people suspected of having links with Freemasons and Jacobins. Consequently Ducros is mentioned in a report by the inquisitorial police of 27th February 1790. This indicates that he frequented the Caffè della Barcaccia in the company of 'French' (ie French-speaking) painters like Simon Denis d'Anvers, Gagneraux (probably Bénigne-Claude, brother of Gustav III's painter), Armand-Charles Caraffe and others (cit. Montaiglon, vol XV, 1906, no 9062).
A note on a drawing in Lausanne dated 18th March 1791, and signed by William Hamilton, specifies that the latter paid Ducros for various drawings obtained in Naples (see Chessex, 1984 (1), p 434).

1792

Ducros resident at the same address (AV, S Lorenzo, 1792, fol 28/v). Kaiserman now in the Via Otto Cantoni (AV, S Lorenzo, 1792, fol 74). After training with Ducros, he set up on his own, collaborated with Bartolomeo Pinelli at the turn of the century and, at the beginning of the nineteenth century, became fashionable as a painter of views.
23rd January: Arrival in Rome of Béat de Hennezel, a typical member of the well-to-do classes of Yverdon. An architect, draughtsman, dilettante and traveller, he kept a detailed journal of his trip to Italy (ACV, P Hennezel), which is in fact a memoir largely re-written after his return. Nevertheless, Hennezel was an eye-witness to this troubled time in Rome, and attention should be paid to his contribution despite some notorious inaccuracies and bias.

May: at the second salon of the Société des Arts de Genève Ducros exhibits four works: *View of Tivoli* and *View of the Colosseum* owned by Monsieur de Tournes, *View of the Arch of Septimius Severus* owned by Monsieur Martin-Sales and *Cascades at Tivoli* owned by Monsieur Tronchin-Calandrini (nos 11, 12, 18 and 19 respectively in the *Notice des tableaux....1792*).

1793

13th January: First uprising against the French in Rome. The diplomat Hugou de Bassville having worn his tricolour rosette too obviously is attacked by a crowd protesting against the new French government. Stabbed, he dies in the night. Most of the French leave Rome in fear of their lives.

21st January: Having visited the Sablet brothers, Sophie-Albertine, sister of Gustav III of Sweden, went to see 'Mr Ducros, painter of water-colour views and landscapes', before visiting Angelica Kauffmann (*Journal of visits made by Her Royal Highness* . . . Royal Bernadotte Archives, Stockholm; reference kindly provided by Birgitta Sandstroem).

6th February: Béat de Hennezel dines with Ducros (ACV, P Hennezel fol 27).

13th February: Hennezel notes that Gagneraux had left Rome, as had the Sablets. This is confirmed by Ducros himself: 'Cardinal Zelada forced me to leave a superb establishment, exiling me from Rome on 12th February '93 at twenty-four hours notice, following the civil troubles which had prevailed after the death of Citizen Bassville. Some people, jealous of my prosperity, described me to the Government as a very dangerous man, attached to the French Republican Party. I was thus obliged to leave in haste, and King Gustav III of Sweden's sister, who was in Rome at the time, was unable to prevent the execution of a sentence dictated by the lies of those who wanted me out of the way in order to build on the debris of my establishment and take my place.' (Letter to the Directory, Naples, 1st April 1799; see Appendix 2). Hennezel confirms that 'Ducros was unable to get his things in any kind of order, and they were left in the hands of the housekeeper and her son, a bad sort' (fol 27). Louis Junod in the catalogue of the Lausanne exhibition of 1953, interprets the French of this last phrase ('à la discretion de sa gouvernante et de son fils, mauvais sujet') and concludes that Ducros had a son of fifteen at the time. The parish registers refute this: they indicate that Ducros lived for several years in the same house as Signora Rosa Crolli, who had a son and daughter, but their father was not Ducros. In 1792 the housekeeper's son, Vicenzo, was thirteen and living alone with his mother, (AV, S Lorenzo, 1792, fol 28/v)

Ducros leaves the Papal States for the Abruzzi, beyond Tivoli. Here he spends several months painting the Liri valley (there are numerous pictures of this region, see cat nos 26–28) 'where he was still active; he even approached the Pope who was most displeased at receiving the person who was involved in the matter, after which he went to Naples. He is believed to be in disgrace for his excessive greed which earned him a mass of enemies there; a group of Italian artists set against him was formed in order to expel him so they could take his place'. (Hennezel, fol 25). As we have already seen, this was what Ducros himself believed. In 1785 De la Rive had written

that Ducros 'was not liked, and everyone feared and avoided him' (Morsier, 1972, p 271). These rumours even reached England, where Sir Richard Colt Hoare full of indulgence for his protégé, attributed his competitors' jealousy to 'his superior merits' (Colt Hoare, 1822, p 83).

7th March: 'Ducros has sent a false sale of his Roman property to a certain Astucci, Prince Borghese's architect [Mario Asprucci (1764–1804), architect of the Temple of Aesculapius in the Borghese Gardens] to rid himself of the artists drawing in his house' (Hennezel fol 29). Ducros stays in exile throughout the summer, on the outer reaches of the Papal States. Stating that he cannot return to Rome he goes to Naples, a city he knows well, where he hopes to find patrons or, at least, customers.

29th June: 'Received from Naples a letter from Ducros, assigning me, in case he had to wait still longer, with sending him the effects remaining in his house, it being for me to arrange for their packing and removal; I passed this letter on to Trippel, the sculptor from Schaffhausen, and he had received a similar one; we agreed that neither of us should take on a task for such a selfish, mean and irksome man; I wrote to him, excusing myself with my lack of practice in the Italian language which would lead to my being deceived' (Hennezel fol 92). One should add that Hennezel considered Kaiserman 'treacherous and dangerous' (fol 6) Sablet is 'treacherous' (fol 7), Gagneraux is 'a bad lot' (fol 24), while Ducros was 'servile' (fol 27), and so on.

1794–98

'The Baron has been out every day since Lady Anne came to Naples. At dinner yesterday, besides the two Swedes, Graft and Ducros were there. All they and the Baron did for three-quarters of an hour was speak ill of the Cavalier Piranesi: and when the servant arrived the Baron stopped, but Ducros went on', (letter from Benedetto Mori to Francesco Piranesi, 8th February, 1794, cit. *Lettera di Francesco Piranesi al Signor Generale D. Giovanni Acton*, [Naples], 1796). The letter concerns spying in which Francesco Piranesi and Baron Armfelt were involved; Ducros seems to have been only a witness.

In a Swiss report of 1794–96 J G Meusel wrote: 'M. Ducros of Yverdon has now settled in Naples after living for some years in Rome. His genius has led him to abandon the business of engraving in which he was occupied, and he has dedicated himself entirely to painting. His speciality is landscapes, for which he has chosen his own style of water-colour. He paints on paper with thick colours in warm and striking tones. His sketches, which are mostly very large, are made with a thick brush producing a fantastic effect which is yet realistic and true to nature. He is paid a great deal for them by connoisseurs on the Grand Tour, especially the English'. (*Neue Miscellaneen*, 1797).

A letter to the editor of the *Journal Litéraire de Lausanne* (December 1796) confirms this: 'DuCros of Yverdon in Switzerland lived in Rome for nearly thirty years; the jealousy of the Italian artists forced him to leave his establishment; he moved to Naples where he remains today'. The English connoisseurs Meusel mentions cannot all be identified, but two of them are known. William Hamilton met Ducros on the artist's trip to the South in 1778, and acquired some of his drawings in 1791.

Gerning records that Ducros water-colours 'are sold at very high prices in England by his protector Hamilton' (*Neuer Teutscher Merkur*, 1798, p 182). Gerning also writes of 'Minister Acton' who 'has a room full of his pictures' (see cat nos 38, 77–79), and in his travel journal notes that 'He has supplied Minister Acton with a room full of varnished gouaches; particularly superb is the launching of a warship against a background of the chestnut-covered slopes of Castellammare, in the presence of the royal family and a large crowd.' (Gerning, 1802, Part II).
Surviving works: Numerous water-colours of the Abruzzi, Naples and Campania, in Lausanne (MCBA), but none dated (see cat nos 26–28 and 30–39)—Six water-colours for Sir John Acton (see cat nos 77–79).

1799

The French troops occupy Naples and Ferdinand IV takes refuge in Sicily. Ducros, in financial difficulties, writes at the beginning of the year to the new Swiss government, as reported in the minutes of the Directoire Helvétique of 6th March 1799: 'Citizen Begoz will recommend Louis Ducroz to the Minister of the Exterior of the Roman Republic, and will ask that he be recommended to the Neapolitan authorities so that he may obtain justice concerning a collapse in which he lost his fortune—he is staying in Naples with the banker Louis Reymond.' (BCU, Fonds La Harpe Ed 3).With French troops nearly everywhere in Europe, Ducros hopes to take advantage by writing a long letter to the Directory in Paris on the 1st April to regain what he had lost on being expelled from Rome. This document is important as one of the few autograph (and partly autobiographical) letters by the Swiss painter (see Appendix 2).
10th June: Ducros' son born in Naples: 'adi 10 Giugno. Luigi Raffaele Gaetano, figlio de Luigi de Gros e Anna da Daychè, coniugi domic. nelle case di Puoti, battezzato dal reverendo Don Gioacchino Zanca coadiutore (delegato), levatrice Antonia De Luca'. (Parish of S. Giuseppe a Chiaja, Baptismal Register, 1779).
When the Bourbons return Ducros has to leave Naples after being denounced as a Jacobin by the architect Pietro Martorana. This is recorded in a note in the Neapolitan archives: 'A Swiss artist of the first order, called Louis Du Cros, has been denied to the city of Naples today, because Martorana has accused him of Jacobinism, and he is now in Rome' (report from the Duca di Campochiaro, minister, on the subject of the architect D. Pietro Martorana, 12th July 1806, Archivio di Stato di Napoli, Min. Interno, Inv. 1, fasc. 972, fol 134).

1800–1801

5th–6th June: Sale of Lord Cawdor's collection in London, including twelve Ducros water-colours, probably first bought by John Campbell on his trip to Italy in 1784 or 1786–88 (see Russell, 1984, p 1746).
8th June: 'Nollekens told me Lord Cawdor collection of works of art sold very well. A drawing of Du Cros for which His Lordship had paid 25 guineas sold for 101 guineas (K Garlick & A Macintyre, ed, *The Diary of Joseph Farington*, 1978, vol IV p 1403.)
November 1800 – May 1801: Ducros in Malta. 'I have been taken to Malta now to paint views for General Graham who has conquered this place' (letter from Ducros to Sir Richard Colt Hoare, 22nd December, 1800. See Appendix 1). Thomas Graham (later Lord Lynedoch) was sent to Malta in November 1799 with the English garrison from Messina to blockade the harbour of Valletta, then occupied by the French. The blockade lasted until 4th September 1800. After Bonaparte's troops had surrendered, Brigadier-General Graham returned to Messina. As Ducros wrote that he arrived at the beginning of November, the two men must have met in Messina in the second half of September or in October. According to Ducros, two of his large drawings reached Lord Elgin that year. Elgin is said to have asked for 'the monuments of the Roman Empire, as Don Tito Lussier had painted those of the Levantine for him'. (Appendix 1).
Surviving works: Five views of Valletta from the Bayfordbury collection, sold Christie's 1945, bought by the National Art Collections Fund and donated to the National Museum of Fine Arts, Valletta. One inscribed: '*Veduta depinta/la viglia dalla/Festa delle palme/in Malta/1800 da Louis DuCros/Pittore Helveti.*'
—Numerous water-colours of Malta (many taken from large paintings) and numerous drawings, tracings, etc., Lausanne (MCBA).
—*Panorama of Malta, viewed from the English quarter at Gudia*, (79 × 211 cm), water-colour, Musée National, on loan to the Château de Wildegg, Switzerland, showing the courtyard front of the Villa Bettina at Gudia, property of Baron Gino Trapani Galea Feriol.

1802

1st May: 'Ducros is in Naples, where I intend going to see him' (Bridel, *Etrennes Helvétiennes*, 1803).

1804

18th March: Ducros in Naples, invited by the priest Daniel-Alexandre Chavannes, on behalf of the Société d'Emulation de Lausanne, to return to Switzerland and establish a drawing school. (*Journal de la Société . . .*, 1841, p 29)

1805

8th January: Ducros writes from Naples to Councillor Lambert requesting him to obtain a house from the government of the Vaud canton, where he could gather together 'the precious things he has in the way of drawings, paintings and plaster casts of antiquities, also to provide accommodation for a small drawing academy' (ACV, register of the Council of State and the indexes of the legislative department, 4th and 6th February 1805).
9th February: The government authorises Lambert to reply to Ducros, stating that 'the government will be delighted to see him retire to his country, and use his talents for the profit of his fellow citizens; a room in the college at Lausanne will be obtained for the storage of his plaster casts, drawings and paintings, and effort will generally be made in order to further his enterprise.' (ACV, register, 9th February 1805). Ducros does not seem to have followed up this letter.
In the summer Schlegel notified Goethe that Ducros was in Naples: 'S Denis and Ducros are staying in Naples, another source of natural beauties . . . Ducros takes inspiration from his journeys in southern Italy, Sicily and Malta for his large water-colour compositions, attractively

15

novel, and representing ruins, seascapes and cliffs (Felsen-Partieen). (Schlegel, 1846–74, IX, p 257).

1806

Ducros resident in Rome.
14th March: Joseph Farington records a discussion on the relative merits of oil and water-colour painting, giving the works of Ducros as examples (op cit, vol VII p 2691) Giuseppe Antonio Guattani, in the second volume of his *Memorie enciclopediche romane* (1807) devotes a long article to 'Signor Luigi Du Cros, painter of water-colour landscapes, a genre he may claim to have fathered and propagated in Rome'. He writes of recent works seen in Ducros' studio, particularly those commissioned by Prince Friedrich von Sachsen-Gotha: *Ponte Lucano* and *Grotte des Pages à Malte*.
Guattani's article is followed by a letter from 'Monsieur Ducros, Swiss landscape painter, Rome, 5th September, 1806', in which he hopes to demonstrate the superiority of water-colour.
Surviving work: Grotte des Pages à Malte, s.d., water-colour, gouache and oil, commission from Friedrich von Sachsen-Gotha, at the castle of Gotha until the Second World War and since 1957 in the Neue Pinakothek, Munich (Hardtwig, 1978, pp 65–68), see cat no 50.

1807

Ducros returns to Switzerland, living first with his brother, Francois-Barthélemy in the small town of Nyon on the banks of Lake Léman between Geneva and Lausanne.
28th October: Ducros obtains exemption from paying tolls on the 'two chests weighing 975 pounds and filled partly with studies, sketches and white paper for his drawings, which he has had delivered by way of the Simplon Pass, and then by water from Vevey to Nyon' (ACV, register 28th October 1807). He only receives the rest of his effects the following summer: 'The pictures coming here from my studio are at this moment in Milan', he wrote on 22nd June, 1808 (ACV, dossier K XIII/63). Ducros first approaches Geneva, where he tries to re-establish links with the artists De la Rive, Saint-Ours, Massot, Bouvier and Töpffer and with families likely to buy from him, such as the Eynards, Chavannes, Châtelains and Duvals, as becomes clear from the few letters preserved from this period in Geneva (BPU, manuscript department).
30th November: The Société des Arts de Genève appoints Ducros an honorary member along with Madame Vigée-Lebrun and Baron de Strogonoff. The *Gazette de Lausanne* reports the event: 'He displays various fine collections of views of Rome, Naples, Malta and Sicily; last summer he painted various subjects in these beautiful regions and will exhibit them next spring' (18th December 1807).

1808

Ducros sends several petitions to the government, asking for funds to open a drawing school. In the summer he moves to Lausanne, considering it a better base for his activities, but he receives only a small subsidy for teaching private individuals. Several ladies come to paint with Ducros, as well as a local nobleman, Sigmund Effinger von Wildegg who took fifty lessons between December 1808 and December 1809 (ACV, Sévery papers, Effinger von Wildegg's notebooks). Wildegg's copies of paintings by Ducros (carefully noted in this book) are to be found attributed to Ducros in various Swiss collections.
Ducros grows insistent with the government and even has a *mémoire* printed, an artistic manifesto in which he suggests the founding of an Academy of Painting and Sculpture, with himself as director (cit. Hugli, 1983, pp 104–106).
Surviving works: Six large water-colours of Swiss subjects, various drawings, copies and sketches, Lausanne (MCBA).

1809

Ducros, tired of the resistance to his ideas in Lausanne and struck by the death of his friend J-P Saint-Ours (9th April 1809), writes to the painter De la Rive: 'Geneva did not know this great man, who should have had a good pension and been educating pupils worthy of him. I could say a thousand things to you about this, being myself sadly reduced to giving lessons after my brilliant success in the south; the gentle veils of the sunset obscure the fleeting rays, and night is approaching with giant steps . . .I often think of you and of the golden age of our picturesque travels in Savoy and Rome. I am quietly preparing for my visit to the eternal landscapes' (BPU, 17th May 1809, MS.2399, letter written on an engraving of the *Temple of the Sibyl*, reproduced Chessex, 1982, fig 7).
In the summer Ducros exhibits in Bern to great acclaim the works he had brought back from Italy. He is supported in Bern by the collector and art dealer Sigmund Wagner, who told the painter David Hess about his enthusiasm for Ducros' work in a letter of 17th September 1809 (cit. Neujahrsblatt, 1899). The exhibition proves to be so successful that the authorities of the city of Bern invite Ducros to become Professor of Painting at the Académie (Staatsarchiv Bern, Manual der Akademischen Kuratel, 9th September 1809).

1810

Ducros, delighted to accept this nomination, is due to take up the post on 1st April when he is struck down by an attack of apoplexy and dies in Lausanne on 18th February, in his sixty-second year.

P.C.

16

Historical and Biographical Notes

Pierre Chessex

The formative years in Switzerland (1760–76)

Ducros spent his childhood and adolescent years in Yverdon on the shores of Lake Neuchâtel. This small town of about 2000 inhabitants, then under the control of Bern, possessed a flourishing economy based upon textiles and paper industries established by Huguenot refugees. The intellectual community and local printing industry played an important part in spreading Enlightenment ideas around both Switzerland and parts of Europe. A notable contribution was made by Fortunato Bartolomeo De Felice, who settled in Yverdon in 1762 and there published forty-two volumes of his *Encylopédie ou Dictionnaire universel raisonné des connaissances humaines*[1]. He dedicated the work to the Bernese scholar Albrecht von Haller, author of *Les Alpes* (1732), a much translated and published poem in which the Alps were presented as a kind of Utopia, as the last bastion of Nature and Humanity in their intact state. Its wide appeal, and the success of the Genevan Jean-Jacques Rousseau's *Nouvelle Héloïse* (1761), made a decisive contribution to a new vision of Switzerland and of nature in general.

The end of the Seven Years War in 1763 enabled travellers of all nationalities to move freely around the Continent once again. Switzerland came to feature on the itinerary of the Grand Tour and *Kavalierreise*. In response to demand from travellers, local artists began to paint water-colours of landscapes and rustic genre scenes illustrating regional costume. Workshops were established in which the outlines of the most picturesque landscapes were engraved and then painted in water-colour and gouache.[2] Bern was one of the main centres for the production of these views, and in 1766 Johann Ludwig Aberli (1723–86) received a patent in the city for making prints of Swiss views using a process named after him. Ducros had the *manière Aberli* in mind when he formed a partnership with the Italian engraver Giovanni Volpato in Rome around 1780.

In his foreword to a collection of Swiss views,[3] Aberli describes a journey he made in 1774: 'The presence of nature must stimulate and excite us; for this sort of sketch drawn, or better painted, on the spot takes on a truthful character which can never be approached by even the best imitation made after the event. . . . I know full well that nature everywhere offers things which may be used to good advantage with some taste and discernment, but I am convinced that in this regard Switzerland is worthy of preference, particularly in the great variety of subjects to be found there, often gathered together in a small space. On the one hand there are wild scenes, more formidable than anywhere else owing to the greater height of our mountains; on the other hand there are the beautiful plains, extensive enough to be reminiscent of views of the Netherlands, and there are even waterscapes on the large lakes; the landscape artist can therefore easily find models for his compositions in every genre. On our travels it sometimes happened that both of us would cry out at the same time: *Salvator Rosa! Poussin! Saveri! Ruisdael!* or *Claude (Lorrain)!*, according to whether the subjects before our eyes reminded us of the manner and choice of one or other of the masters named.'

Although Ducros must have seen engravings by the Bernese *Kleinmeister* in Yverdon, he could not have studied there the great masters of the past to whom Aberli refers. In order to do more than study engravings after the old masters he needed to go to a large town, but Lausanne had neither a school of drawing, art academy, nor any large private collections in the middle of the eighteenth century and on the whole the arts were not encouraged there. To make a career an artist had to go abroad. The Sablet brothers, for example, went to Paris, and then Rome; Benjamin Bolomey went to Paris, before settling in The Hague where he became painter to Stadhouder William V of Orange; Michel-Vincent Brandoin was called *l'Anglais* after studying water-colour painting with Paul Sandby in England. Ducros, possibly uncertain about his career, went to Geneva.

Geneva lacked an official art academy and any aspiring artist had to become an apprentice, as did J F Liotard and J A Linck who worked for engravers. Alternatively, men like J P Saint-Ours and J L Agasse left for Paris. A school of drawing had been founded in Geneva in 1751, but this was vocational in character, training its pupils for the *Fabrique* where craftsmen produced the watches, enamels and chintzes for which Geneva was known abroad.[4]

Private teaching offered another option. Ducros placed himself under Nicolas Henri Joseph Fassin, the *Chevalier de Fassin* (1728–1811).[5] During his stay in Rome in the 1760s this rather uninspired artist from Liège came into contact with Erdmannsdorf and advised him on acquisitions for the Wörlitz Palace. Fassin stayed in Geneva from 1769–70 and collaborated with an important local collector, François Tronchin (1704–98). This merchant banker had a predilection for Dutch and Flemish painting[6] and became famous for selling his first collection to Catherine the Great in 1770. He bought in Paris, Amsterdam and The Hague, choosing works by artists such as Berchem, Metsu and Wouwerman. These he displayed in his house, *Les Délices* which had formerly belonged to Voltaire. Many famous people visited his gallery, including Voltaire himself, Grimm, Madame d'Epinay and many of Geneva's young artists came to copy works in the collection. Under Tronchin's patronage Fassin opened a private academy in Geneva which Ducros, Jean-Daniel Huber (the son of Huber-Voltaire), Louis-Auguste Brun (Marie-Antoinette's painter) and others attended.

Having learned his basic craft, Ducros then followed Fassin to Flanders. Nothing is known about this stay, but a report by the Genevan painter Pierre-Louis de la Rive (1753–1819) gives an idea of the direction of the Chevalier's teaching: 'M. Ducros of Yverdun, who has also taken up painting, and who had been in Flanders for a year with M. de Fassin, came back at this time to settle in Geneva and copy pictures. We took up the palette the same day; he knew a little more than I; he had copied several of his master's drawings, and was a few years older than I. In my extreme ignorance I attached myself to this still very slim reed and we started to copy, copy, copy. We particularly admired Berghem, and this master, full of talent and truth, became for us the model of the most sublime perfection in art. We also respected Wouvermans and Both, Ruysdaal etc. . . . This life began in the spring of 1773. The following year, in September, Messieurs Girod and Ducros suggested a journey to Savoy to sketch from nature. We went to Annecy, Alby, Rumilly, Seyssel, and at the end of three weeks I brought back some bad water-colours which seemed like masterpieces to me and of which I have never been able to make the slightest use. I did not know how to be discerning, I had seen too little; but a true talent, a little tact and feeling would have made up for this lack of experience; my two companions hardly knew any more than me; one was simply an amateur looking only for amusement and diversion; the other was an artist making a start, hesitant, uncertain, but an indefatigable worker with an ardent desire to make his way and his fortune. I followed them like a sheep, with no opinion of my own; if they set to work, I set to work; if the plan was to leave, I left; in short, I was an absolute nothing. We came back to the studio to copy. The following year we made another little study trip which was troubled by continuous rain; we brought nothing back, and this life continued into the summer of 1776'.[7] De la Rive is virtually the only source for Ducros' years in Geneva before he left for Rome (fig 1) and no signed and dated work from this period has yet been found.[8]

The influence of Fassin and the Northern School paintings of the Galerie Tronchin was clearly significant in Ducros' early years, and was strengthened by his reading of the *Lettre sur le paysage* (1770) by another Swiss, Salomon Gessner. But other factors came into play, and help us to understand why Ducros later specialized in topographical landscapes.

In the middle of the eighteenth century there was more collaboration in Geneva between scientists and artists than anywhere else. The illustration of scientific works was one of the essential openings for artists who, having remained in Switzerland, lacked commissions from the aristocracy and the Church. Marc-Théodore Bourrit (1739–1819) drew the valleys of Chamonix and Mont-Blanc and published his *Description des glacières, glaciers et amas de glaces du Duché de Savoie* (1773) before working with A-W Töpffer on the illustrations for Horace-Bénédict de Saussure's *Voyage dans les Alpes*. Henrik Ploetz (1748–1830) the Danish miniaturist, painter of enamels and friend of Ducros, illustrated the works of Charles Bonnet, the celebrated naturalist, patron of Ducros and author of an essay entitled *Contemplation de la Nature* (1764). Bonnet recommended close study of nature as the only means of discovering and conveying 'truth'. This fervent quest was shared by Ducros and other young painters in Geneva, including Huber, De la Rive,

Agasse and Töpffer. A few years later Ducros wrote to Bonnet: 'Ah! How I prefer to be beneath the cascades of Tivoli at sunrise where Newton could split light without a prism. . . . Not content simply to see this wild beauty and go into ecstasies before it, I have conceived the daring plan of perpetuating its image; my pencils will dare to fix on paper these foaming waves and the infinite variations undergone by the supple, fluid water as it squeezes between rocks, flooding them, pressing against them from every direction, and sending flying above their crests its eddying mist, rising like a cloud as if to conceal from view the depths of its chasms; how wonderful it is to study nature; who knows these pleasures better than you, Monsieur?'[9]

This desire to analyse nature probably explains why Ducros was never tempted by idyllic or historical landscapes. Ever since his time in Geneva Ducros was at ease when surrounded by nature. De la Rive wrote in his autobiography of the 'obsession inspired in me by Ducros of always doing wash water-colours on the spot'.[10] The Swiss painter developed this technique in Italy and it made his name.

The Italian years: Ducros as a landscape artist, engraver and dealer

'At this time the great painters were in the forefront of public opinion; they seemed almost unassailable: all paths to fame appeared to be blocked. Mengs, Angelica and Battoni were pre-eminent in historical painting; Hamilton in pastels; Hackert and Moore in landscapes; while Fidance challenged Vernet himself in the minor genre of seascape painting. What could one man alone do? Sensibility and imagination came to his aid'.[11]

This observation, made in the year of Ducros' arrival in Rome, only mentions the leading artists in the city. In 1787 Aloys Hirt listed 400 Italian and 163 foreign artists living there. Some of these did not need to worry about money as they either had personal fortunes, a patron or enjoyed a royal stipend (as did the artists at the French Academy). Catholic artists could make their way with religious paintings commissioned by the Church, others might work on large decorative projects for the Vatican, Palazzo Chigi or the Villa Borghese. But many young artists arriving in Rome had to struggle to find work; Gagneraux painted fans and then copied ancient bas-reliefs for engravers;[12] others copied famous works for the tourists.

Ducros was lucky enough to be employed by a Dutchman travelling to the Kingdom of the Two Sicilies, and this was to have a decisive effect on his career. This 'Grand Tour' of 1778 took him to southern Italy, Sicily and Malta, where he painted topographical views of Mediterranean landscapes and ancient monuments. The drawings he took back with him (see cat nos 51–53) provided a repertoire of ruins, views and picturesque scenes which he later put to great use (fig 2).

fig. 2   Ducros, *Vue du château de Capo di Monte, Naples*, Rijksprentenkabinet, Amsterdam.

Ducros' association with Giovanni Volpato

At this time landscape was considered a minor genre in academic circles, even though it had long been basic to an artist's training. On returning to Rome Ducros realised that his only hope of employment lay in selling picturesque souvenirs to foreign visitors, so he went into business with the engraver Giovanni Volpato (1732–1803), a man with a significant reputation in Rome at the time.[13] His hand-coloured prints of Raphael's *loggie* and *stanze* at the Vatican were widely known in the 1770's. J H Meyer, Goethe's collaborator, declared in *Winckelmann und sein Jahrhundert* (1805) that Volpato had helped to spread the gospel of good taste in the civilised world. The prints also attracted the favour of Pius VI, under whose protection Volpato carried out archaeological excavations at Frascati, the Baths of Caracalla and around the Arch of Titus with Gavin Hamilton,[14] which brought him fame and fortune. Volpato had trained at the Calcografia Remondini, then with Bertolozzi and Wagner in Venice. His association with Ducros began in 1779–80 and represents a fusion between the tradition of large print reproductions and the small coloured engravings of the Swiss *Kleinmeister* with whom Ducros had come into contact when young.

The novelty of Ducros and Volpato's *Vues de Rome et de ses environs* (1780) lay principally in the fact that they were contemporary views produced on a very large format. They etched the outlines of the site to be depicted, paying particular attention to the architecture, which was drawn with great precision, indicating here and there the values of light and shade by several treatments with acid which eats away at the plate to a greater or lesser depth, and sometimes retouching it with dry-point for the details. Certain parts— foliage, the water of the fountains and cascades—were not always engraved as the print had to be coloured. Once the prints had been taken, they were coloured with water-colour and sometimes a light application of gouache, by assistants or students working in the studio, using as a basis the original drawing which they had in front of them. Since the lines of the engraving are covered with paint the prints have a quality which can make them pass for original hand-coloured drawings. This confusion has certainly been sustained on occasions, as much by the dealer—who can thus ask more for it—as by the buyer, who can pass off the print on his wall as an original water-colour.[15]

The series of *Vues de Rome* is mentioned in Meusel's *Miscellaneen* (1781): 'M Ducros of Yverdon, who has gained an excellent reputation in Rome, is working in collaboration with M Volpato on a collection of illuminated views of Rome: twelve pieces in the format of the *School of Athens* are finished, as are twelve of medium size. M Ducros engraves the copper plates marking only the outlines, then, under his and M Volpato's direction, the engravings are illuminated by young artists with the result that they are barely distinguishable from original drawings'.[16] Peter Birmann (1758–1844), the young Swiss who worked in Volpato's studio from 1782, saw things differently: 'Ducros, in collaboration with the celebrated engraver Volpato, had an art business which he ran almost alone, while his associate guided and supervised the engravers and painters in a superb studio' (*Neujahrsblatt*, 1859).

It is difficult to know exactly who did what as these prints are rarely lettered. The two artists generally signed between the margins: *Ducros et Volpato f. Roma* or simply *Ducros et Volpato*, sometimes with a date between 1780 and 1784, the signature often preceded by a number, with the title written in ink or engraved on a separate piece of paper and pasted on.

In 1782 Ducros moved to a gallery and studio in the Strada della Croce where he remained until 1793. Here his interests grew more diverse. In his letter to the Directory (see Appendix 2) he states that he had 'a collection of coloured views . . . which were a profitable employment for [his] firm'. His own prints were coloured by assistants but he also illuminated and sold engravings by other painters, as is clear from the *Catalogue des vues de Rome* which contains subjects he never painted (notably nos 22, 23, 36, 37, 39 and 40 from the large views, and nos 7 and 11 of the small ones). Moreover, the Lausanne studio collection includes prints by F Piranesi after Desprez, some of which bear the phrase *se vend chez Ducros*.[17] Volpato and Piranesi followed the same practice and sold coloured prints on which the artist's name does not appear,[18] making attribution even more complicated.

The ambiguous status of these etchings[19] was one reason why they received a cool response from some collectors. As early as 1780 Roland de la Platière remarked that prints like these were not worthy of mention and were suitable only for the English who 'are mad about them'.[20] Sir Richard Colt Hoare praised Ducros' water-colours in his *History of Modern Wiltshire* (1822), but did not even mention the two hand-coloured etchings he owned (*Forum of Nerva with the Colonacce; The Arch of Titus*). Even today little importance is attached to them and there is hardly any literature on the subject. But they did have their moment of glory. The series of views by Ducros and Volpato had numerous buyers, some of whom were people of importance, such as King Stanislas-August Poniatowski (prints now destroyed, one remaining at the university library in Warsaw), Catherine the Great (two virtually complete sets at the Hermitage) and Gustav III of Sweden and his courtiers (several sets in Stockholm, at the Kungl. Husgeradskammern, the Nationalmuseum and the Palace of Drottningholm).

Ducros cannot have been too concerned at this lack of total success, as he remarked, this was 'just one branch of business that he had added to his other affairs', which included 'his very considerable commissions for paintings', by which he meant original water-colours (see Appendix 2).

Problems with dating

Ducros rarely signed his original works and dated them even less frequently. Some of the small water-colours and the prints bear dates between 1779 and 1784, but large paintings with dates are few in number. The latter include a large *Roman landscape* (oil, 1780, Kunstmuseum, Bern) *Grand Duke Paul in the Forum,* (oil, 1782, Pavlovsk Palace, Leningrad), *Waterfalls at Terni* (water-colour, 1786, Rome art market, 1983), *Pius VI visiting the drainage works at the Pontine Marshes* (oil, 1786, Museo di Roma, cat no 55), *View of Valletta* (water-colour and oil, 1800, Museum of Fine Arts, Valletta), and *Grotte des Pages à Malte* (water-colour and oil, 1806, Neue Pinakothek, Munich).

The large record books marked *LRDC* that the painter mentioned in his will have not been located. Although the Lausanne drawings bear dated watermarks these are only *termini post quem*. Historical information on certain commissions and the reminiscences of the many visitors to his Rome studio in the years 1783 to 1793 provide the only certain evidence for undated works. Dating is further complicated by Ducros' systematic use of tracings or *lucido* which he used to repeat subjects years later. In Lausanne there are about a hundred, many marked with technical notes.[21] Tracing was much used by artists in Rome to copy works for anthologies[22] and also by landscape artists such as J V Nicolle[23] and L-F Cassas.[24]

The large-scale water-colours (1784–1806)

Ducros' first large paintings were the oils commissioned by Pius VI and Grand Duke Paul of Russia (see cat nos 55, 56); there is no evidence to suggest that he painted large water-colours before 1784. He probably made his water-colours slightly larger between 1782 and 1784, no doubt encouraged by the success of his large hand-coloured prints and the example of J P Hackert, John 'Warwick' Smith and John Robert Cozens.[25] Several drawings from these years show the artist working out of doors, a theme common in the history of painting,[26] although the size of the paper on the sketcher's lap is unusual. For example, in a water-colour of the interior of the Colosseum (fig 3) an artist is shown drawing on a portfolio about 60 × 100 cm, far bigger than the usual sketch-book. The studio collection contains no sketch-books, while the average size of Ducros' drawings is 55 × 75 cm. Amateurs' portfolios are different in size and these large drawings were not intended for them, so they must have been intended for display.

Ducros pasted his drawings onto canvas and then mounted them on a stretcher in order to preserve and exhibit them in his studio. He does not seem to have participated in public exhibitions (except for those held in Geneva in 1789 and 1792), but depended upon the common practice of opening his studio to visitors. Ducros clearly wanted to compete with painters in oils, as can be inferred from the fact that these water-colours were generally framed and put under glass.[27] Some water-colours are on a single sheet of paper such as the *Arch of Constantine* (cat no 2), but Ducros usually had to stick several sheets together to obtain the desired format. This was standard from 1784–5 and enabled him to paint landscapes on an exceptional scale.

Travellers and writers visiting his studio were impressed, particularly by his depiction of waterfalls. An article in *Memorie per le Belle Arti* (April 1785) describes his waterfalls of the Anio at Tivoli and the Velino at Terni: 'As the water cascades precipitously from on high, it disperses into an immense quantity of the tiniest drops, which spread like a white mist, veiling surrounding objects and blurring them, making the colours and outlines unclear. This observation, neglected by many, has not escaped Monsieur Ducros who has imitated to perfection the moist and misty air, and has rendered with the very greatest success the haziness with which we see everything enveloped in such vapours'.

A few years later Bridel recalled how: 'Ducros observed that we never see objects through a pure medium, but through an atmosphere which, although vaporous to a greater or lesser extent, always modifies colours; a delicate modification to be sure, but without awareness of it true colouring would not exist'. To obtain such effects it was necessary to have a complete mastery of painting techniques, as Bridel realized: 'It was not enough simply to have an idea, one had to execute it; execution was difficult. *Oil* gives smooth tints on a shiny surface and has nothing soft to its nature; pastel is better suited to producing this effect, but cannot be fixed and soon deteriorates; for every true tint in *gouache* there are ten false ones; he used *water-colour* and painted on paper. Water-colour is a form of painting in which natural colours made from the saps of various plants are used; they are only very lightly gummed and thus preserve the freshness, the variety, the softness and all the *tone* of nature. By using them landscape can be expressed with great truth, light can be intelligently broken down, the movement of water can be indicated, the moist dust rising from the bottom of waterfalls, the morning haze, the evening mists, in short all those elements which pass almost unperceived, and which together are to be thanked for the beauty of a landscape' (*Etrennes Helvétiennes*, 1790).

Ducros' waterfalls may have been a great success, but ancient monuments were also important in his landscapes. Having assimilated the styles of Panini, Piranesi and Hubert Robert, he formulated his own. Trained as a topographical view painter, he gained experience at observing nature directly and with precise and authentic detail. But he also attached great importance to composition in order to give his landscapes greater strength; he played with perspective through oblique views, stretched space and used multiple vanishing points. Historians have tended to over-estimate the topographical precision of Ducros' landscapes, and regarded them as primarily of documentary interest. But although *vedute ideate* and *capricci* are relatively rare in his work (see cat nos 24 and 36) a great deal of imagination came into play in his landscapes along with scrupulous attention to detail. Ducros did not look at ancient monuments as an archaeologist, but as a lover of natural beauty. For him, nature and history are closely linked. Whether depicting the inside of the Colosseum, a stream winding through the Abruzzi or the interior of the Villa of Maecenas he was really concerned with the poetry of a grotto, playing with light and shade and modulating colours. With his mastery of water-colour techniques Ducros achieved striking effects by superimposing tones, particularly in the back-lighting of foliage and creating of half-shadows. Figures and gouache heightening were then added to enliven and balance the composition.

Figures

From very early in his career Ducros used assistants to draw figures[28] following a practice common in Rome in the eighteenth century.[29] Among Ducros' contemporaries J P Hackert had difficulty in painting figures and sought assistance, while in Geneva A W Töpffer, Firmin Massot and Jacques-Laurent Agasse collaborated on pictures, painting the landscape, figures and animals respectively.

The work of at least three hands can be distinguished in Ducros' figures. First there is his own, to be seen in everything before 1783, including the prints. From the Rome years there is a hand similar to David in style, (see, for example, *Interior of the Colosseum*, cat no 4). Finally, in most of the works from the Neapolitan period we find the most elegant, expressive and common of the three, that of the mysterious 'Venetian' assistant mentioned by J Isaac Gerning.[30] Several of the drawings in Lausanne bear inscriptions on the reverse which probably date from the first inventories made after Ducros' death. Some read 'figures by Pinelli', others 'figures by Mazzola'. The first attribution must result from confusion with Bartolomeo Pinelli (1781–1835) who assisted Kaiserman around 1805 in Rome, and whose style is not evident in the figures painted for Ducros.[31] The question of Mazzola is more complex. Various Swiss museums, particularly Basel and Bern, contain Italian figure studies which are stylistically close and one is signed *Mazzola fec: Roma* (see fig 4). This belonged to Sigmund Wagner, a Bernese friend of Ducros. These studies are by the same hand as the figures painted for Ducros, and a drawing in the same style in Lausanne, traditionally called *M Ducros perd son chapeau*, (see fig 5) is marked *Mazuola*. Could this be Giuseppe Mazzola di Valduggia (1748–1838) who worked in Rome under Mengs and who was to become court painter to Victor-Amédée of Savoy? It is conceivable that after he became an historical painter he condemned his 'hackwork' as Ducros' figure painter as all the drawings by Mazzola preserved at the Pinacoteca di Varallo are purely historical in subject and bear no relation to those in Lausanne.[32]

fig. 4
Mazzola,
Figure Studies,
Kunstmuseum, Bern.

fig. 5
Mazzola,
M. Ducros perd son chapeau, Lausanne
(MCBA).

The mystery may be solved one day, but for the moment we can only note that the figures in Ducros' landscapes are above all elements in the composition. Ducros decided on their position within the arrangement of the picture and left appropriate spaces on his paper. The figures were then placed with great care on the compositional axes of the paintings and painted on in bright gouache, contributing to the vibrant colouring of these works.

The views of Sicily and Malta

The Chronology explains the circumstances in which Ducros made a series of views of Sicily around 1789 for publication in association with P P Montagnani. To the list of works sold in the Strada della Croce (see Appendix 2) Ducros attached a prospectus for twenty-four views of Sicily, which suggests that they were published in 1799. In the fourth volume of his *Manuel des amateurs* of 1800 (ad vocem Montagnani) Huber is quite specific on the subject: 'They have just published a little prospectus in which they announce that 24 views of Sicily and the Island of Malta are to be presented to the public by subscription'. Ducros also mentioned this subscription in December 1800 (letter to Sir Richard Colt Hoare, Appendix 1), specifying that the views had yet to be engraved.

The only known dated work depicting Sicily is a *View of Catania and Mount Etna* (1789).[33] The studio collection in Lausanne contains a portfolio of works without inventory numbers including pen drawings, tracings, reverse proofs of etchings and their counter-proofs. These depict various sites in Sicily such as Messina, Catania, Palermo, Segesta, Selinunte, Agrigento, Syracuse and Taormina. Also known are a *View of the Palazzina at Messina after the earthquake* (Geneva art market, 1983), a *veduta ideata* with the Temple of Concord, Taormina and Mount Etna (private collection, Geneva) and *The Greek Theatre at Syracuse* (Victoria and Albert Museum, see cat no 76). These landscapes may be dated between 1789 and 1793.[34]

Documentary sources contradict each other over the publication of prints taken from drawings of Sicily. According to Chavannes (*Journal*, 1835) 'the political storms which were soon to rise posed an insurmountable obstacle to the planned publication'. Joubert speaks of a 'collection which must be counted among the finest products of engraving; the brilliance of the burin matches that of the colour, and this work must place the artist in the front rank of modern landscapists'.[35] Joubert must have been mistaken—especially as he mentions the burin when Ducros in fact made etchings. It is most likely that only a few isolated prints were published, with Ducros selling his original water-colours to travellers. The large views of Malta (see cat nos 43–50) remained with Ducros, and he took them back to Lausanne at the end of his life; only one etching was made (see cat no 49).

Distribution of the works

'These works grace the finest private collections in England and Russia, his relations with these two countries having been sustained over many years. True, he is little known in France; but many artists and celebrated connoisseurs of that country (we could mention the famous DAVID) to whom we have shown our drawings have placed them in the front rank of works of this kind'.[36]

At the beginning of the nineteenth century Ducros was often mentioned in the press and his works were admired by art-lovers in Geneva (Bruun Neergaard, 1802), Naples (Gerning, 1802; Schlegel, 1805), Rome (Fernow, 1809), and Paris (according to the *Journal d'Alméras* in 1824 Count Sommariva had a room full of them). In London his name appears several times in discussions of water-colour landscape painting recorded by Joseph Farington[37] and his works went for astronomical sums, as in the sale of Lord Cawdor's collection in June 1800. In his will Ducros cited creditors in London, St. Petersburg and Palermo as being listed in his record book but this is now unlocated.

Clearly Ducros' work was widely known in Europe around 1800.[38] In Rome and Naples he came into contact with the most distinguished British, French, German and Italian painters in water-colour. The exchange of ideas and mutual influence cannot be evaluated easily today. Ducros' work has points in common with the landscapes of L F Cassas and J P Houel, the views of Tito Lusieri and Hackert, and the water-colours of John 'Warwick' Smith and John Robert Cozens. This exhibition should give scholars and art-lovers alike the opportunity to appreciate the true quality of a Swiss painter who, in his time, was the object of more enthusiasm in England than in his own country.

1   *Fortunato Bartolomeo De Felice, editore illuminista (1723–89), una mostra da Yverdon a Milano*, Biblioteca Nazionale Braidense, Milan, 1983.
2   *Maegtige Schweiz. Inspirationer fra Schweiz 1750–1850*, Thorvaldsen Museum, Copenhagen, 1973; *The Alps in Swiss Painting*, Odakyn Grand Gallery, Tokyo, 1977 and The Grisons Museum of Art, Chur, 1977.
3   Collection/de quelques vues/dessinées en Suisse/d'après nature/par J-L Aberli, A Berne,/chez Rieter 1782.
4   For the artistic situation in Geneva see: J J Rigaud, *Renseignements sur les Beaux-Arts à Genève*, Geneva, 1876; Mauro Natale, *Le goût et les collections d'art italien à Genève du XVIIIe au XXe siècle*, Geneva, MAH, 1980; Anne de Herdt, *Dessins genevois de Liotard à Hodler*, Musée Rath, Geneva, 1984.
5   Denis Coekelberghs, *Les peintres belges à Rome de 1700 à 1830*, Brussels & Rome, 1976, pp 301–304.
6   *De Genève à l'Ermitage. Les collections de François Tronchin*, Musée Rath, Geneva, 1974 (introduction by Renée Loche).
7   De la Rive, *Notes diverses qui pourront servir après ma mort*, published as *Notice biographique de M P-L de la Rive, peintre de paysage, membre de la Société des Arts écrite par lui-même*, Geneva (Vignier), 1832.
8   With the possible exception of two compositions with fishermen in the Musée de Berne and a small *Paysage avec une scierie* (33·7 × 48·1 cm), signed but not dated, Nationalmuseum, Stockholm, from the collection of J T Sergel, reproduced in Bjurstrom, 1982, no 938. Sergel left Rome in 1779 and Ducros may have given it to him between 1776 and 1779. It is unlikely that he acquired a non-Italian landscape like this when he accompanied Gustave III to Rome in 1784 when Ducros was at the peak of his career.
9   Rome, 7th July 1783, BPU, MS Bonnet 37.
10   De la Rive, 1832, p 11.
11   Bridel, 1789, *Etrennes Helvétiennes* for 1790.
12   B. Sandstroem, 1981, p 29.
13   Chessex, 1982, pp 47–54 and E Tittoni-Monti, 1983, pp 405–408.
14   Carlo Pietrangeli, *Scavi e scoperte di antichità sotto il pontificato di Pio VI*, second edition, Rome, 1958.
15   'Finally, illumination. This genre combining engraving and drawing has been brought to a high degree of perfection in our time. In this method prints taken from lightly etched plates are carefully coloured. The best of this new genre of illumination is to be found in the architectural pieces of Du Cros and Volpato, Sandby's landscapes and several others' (Huber and Rost, 1797, vol 1). The same passage is also to be found in the *Notizie degli intagliatori* (vol IV, 1808), where the author adds: 'Such are the Swiss views of Aberli.'
16   Meusel, *Miscellaneen*, 1781, p 190.
17   Wollin, 1933, p 32.
18   See the list of works sold by Piranesi in Rome, which includes 'illuminated drawings by Després, Sablet, Ducrot, Panini, etc.', published in Montaiglon, XVII, 1908, no 9842.
19   See van de Sandt, 1980.

20   J-M Roland de la Platière, *Lettres écrites de Suisse, d'Italie, de Sicile et de Malthe en 1776, 1777 et 1778*, vol V, Amsterdam, 1780, p 97.
21   'Bisogna nel lucidarlo in carta buona/alzare di un quadrato e mezzo per poter componerci un primo piano', or again 'Dessin qu'il faut lucidare/demain matin et le coller après diné', etc.
22   Sandstroem, 1981, pp 33, 47.
23   Baudicour, *Le peintre-graveur français continué*, II, 1869, p 309.
24   H Boucher, 'Louis-Francois Cassas', *Gazette des Beaux-Arts*, 1926, pp 51, 219.
25   No reference to a meeting between Ducros and J R Cozens has been found, but it is possible that Smith and Cozens visited Ducros' studio as several reports from travellers between 1784 and 1789 remark on the constant presence of English visitors, including John Ramsay (see Chronology, 1783).
26   Bruno Weber, 'Die Figur des Zeichners in der Landschaft', *Zeitschrift für Schweizerische Archäologie und Kunstgeschichte*, 34 (1977), pp 44–82.
27   Jane Bayard, *Works of Splendor and Imagination: The Exhibition Watercolor, 1770–1870*, Yale Center for British Art, New Haven, 1981, which makes no mention of Ducros.
28   Agassiz, 1927, p 11.
29   Anthony M Clark, 'A Supply of Ideal Figures', *Paragone*, 139 (1961), pp 51–58.
30   'For the figures there is a Venetian assistant he keeps hidden' (Gerning, 1802, II, pp 107–108).
31   Famous for his costumes, brigands, and popular Italian scenes, Pinelli was influenced by the Sablet and Ducros aquatints published around 1782–3.
32   Information kindly provided by Giovanni Romano of the Soprintendenza per i Beni artistici e storici del Piemonte, Turin.
33   Water-colour over pen, 74 × 53.5 cm, Paul Prouté, 1982, Catalogue no 41, as *La côte de Sorrente*. The MCBA in Lausanne has a drawing and a counter-proof of an etching of the same subject and the same size. The Goethe-Museum in Rome has a water-colour painted on the counter-proof of an identical etching, misattributed to Oeser.
34   A set of line drawings of Sicilian monuments at the Musée d'Art et d'Histoire de Genève are copies made by Ducros for Madame Eynard in 1809 (BPU, MS suppl. 1895, fol 338).
35   F E Joubert, *Manuel de l'amateur d'estampes*, I, 1821, p 443, a text consulted by Ticozzi, Gabet, Raabe, De Boni, Bryan, Blanc, Hoefer, Seubert, etc.
36   Chavannes, 1821, p 47.
37   *The Diary of Joseph Farington*, ed. K. Garlick, A. Macintyre & K. Cave, London & New Haven 1978–84, pp 291, 1403, 2691 (11 January 1795, 8 June 1800, 14 March 1806).
38   For the critical literature between 1800 and the present see Chessex, 1982.

Ducros and the British

Lindsay Stainton

On the 3rd January 1787 Philip Secretan, a Swiss visitor to Rome, noted in his diary: 'On leaving my inn, I went to Ducros'—he was surrounded by pictures. Two Englishmen were showering him with praise; I was expecting to meet a compatriot, but I found only a cold producer of landscapes engaged in selling gouaches to the English'.[1] Unfortunately Secretan did not identify Ducros' enthusiastic admirers, and such fleeting references are tantalisingly characteristic of what little can be established about the Swiss artist and his British patrons. With one or two significant exceptions, his name is equally lacking in any eighteenth or nineteenth century account of the development of the British school of landscape painting or in any British account of the continental art of the period. There are however some fragmentary clues which when pieced together give some idea of the British patronage he enjoyed, and of his influence on British landscape art.

Ducros initially settled in Rome in 1776, and in 1778 is recorded as having accompanied, in the capacity of draughtsman, an expedition of a group of Dutch antiquaries to the Kingdom of the Two Sicilies and Malta. Nothing further is known of his activities until 1779 when he began his collaboration with the engraver Giovanni Volpato (see Chronology). Between them they perfected a technique, almost a system of mass-production, for turning out views of Rome and its environs; the essentials of the composition were lightly etched, and these faint outlines extensively reinforced with water-colour and gouache 'in such a way that they are hardly distinguishable from original drawings'.[2] Sometimes, confusingly, the outlines were not etched, but traced and strengthened by hand, giving a spurious impression of originality. The publication of these prints marks the beginning of Ducros' popularity with British visitors to Rome. Previously, travellers in search of inexpensive views to take home as souvenirs had had to depend on the Calcografia, an institution which had accumulated a large collection of engraved plates from the stock of deceased or retired print-publishers. Impressions were taken in accordance with the demand, so that the plates became increasingly worn and had to be reworked; and though the prints were conceived in black and white terms, impressions were often hand-coloured to make them more saleable.[3] It is not surprising, therefore, that when Ducros set up his own studio and shop towards the end of 1781, the success of this venture should have been reflected in the number of contemporary references to him in Italian newspapers and chronicles and in private letters, and in the numerous commissions that he received, notably from British travellers, whose demands both for large-scale water-colours and for coloured engravings was at its height in the middle years of the decade. In the early 1780s, Ducros' name was almost unknown in England, yet he was able to build up a circle of British clients in Rome. Some of them limited their purchases to one or two examples as souvenirs, but others, notably Sir Richard Colt Hoare of Stourhead, became faithful patrons.

The principal intermediary responsible for bringing them into contact with Ducros seems to have been the antiquarian and dealer James Byres (1734–1817).[4] He acted as cicerone to most of those British visitors who subsequently became patrons of Ducros. The artist Thomas Jones, who lived in Italy between 1776 and 1783, gave a description, in his *Memoirs*, of Byres' house in the Strada Paolina where he saw works by those artists for whom Byres acted as agent. Byres 'had his Party among the Artists, and it was customary for every one to present a Specimen of his Abilities to his Protector . . . These specimens were hung up in [the] Rooms of Audience for the inspection of the Cavaliers who came'.[5] An inventory drawn up in May 1790, when Byres was about to leave Rome for good, includes framed prints by Ducros hung in a passage near the drawing-room. That Byres acted as intermediary between Ducros and his customers can be glimpsed from his correspondence; in October 1785, for instance, writing to William Constable about a commission for four of the Ducros/Volpato prints—which incidentally he refers to as 'colour'd drawings'—he expressed the opinion that Ducros has 'carried that stile of painting nearer to perfection than has hitherto been done. It was lucky that the commission came towards the end of the summer, as I had the choice of all that was prepared for the Travellers next winter'.[6] This letter also raises the question of whether patrons always knew if they were getting an original water-colour or a coloured etching. But in an age when copies after the Old Masters had a legitimate status of their own, and when landscape drawings and prints were often regarded as topographical records rather than works of art in their own right, such purist quibbles may have seemed unduly pedantic.

The British patron whose relationship with Ducros is most fully documented is Sir Richard Colt Hoare (1758–1838) of Stourhead, not only one of the most distinguished antiquarians of his generation, but also a collector and an early patron of the young J M W Turner, and himself an enthusiastic amateur draughtsman (he had been a pupil of John 'Warwick' Smith). In 1785 he inherited Stourhead from his grandfather Henry Hoare, the creator of the celebrated landscape gardens there; but in the same year his wife died and he left England to assuage his grief by pursuing his antiquarian studies in Italy. Except for a brief period in 1787, he did not return for six years. After spending the winter of 1785–86 in Naples, he settled in Rome in February 1786. Here he followed established practice in visiting 'the immense labyrinth of antiquities and rarities'[7] under the guidance of a cicerone. His guides were James Byres and his partner Colin Morrison, who, as Colt Hoare's journal and correspondence show, also acted on his behalf as agents for the purchase of books, paintings and casts from the Antique. It was almost certainly through Byres that Colt Hoare was introduced to Ducros, and also to Carlo Labruzzi (unusual among Italian artists in being primarily a water-colourist) and the German-born Philipp Hackert (the most influential landscapist in Rome at this period). As Kenneth Woodbridge has pointed out,[8] Colt Hoare's taste in Old Master paintings was restricted and conventional. His real interests lay in topography and classical history—two passions he was able to combine in his patronage of Ducros and Labruzzi. His appreciation of Italian landscape seems to have been filtered through his knowledge of the remote past, as if he were able to enjoy a scene only by associating it with some historical or mythological event. Thus in November 1789 he set out to study the course of the Appian Way, taking Labruzzi with him to make a series of water-colours (of their kind, among the most remarkable to have been painted in the eighteenth century), with the intention of publishing a series of engravings; but bad weather and Labruzzi's ill-health prevented them from completing the expedition. Colt Hoare's patronage of Ducros can be seen in much the same light: all thirteen landscapes bought for Stourhead between 1786 and 1793 are connected with themes from ancient history or mythology. They include versions of subjects that other English visitors acquired simply because they were spectacularly impressive—the Falls at Terni, for example, or a storm in the Nera valley—but that Colt Hoare valued for their classical and literary associations.

But besides his predilection for Ducros' subject-matter, Colt Hoare was also interested in his techniques. In a letter of February 1787 to his half-brother Hugh, he wrote 'Du Cros an artist— whom I think I mentioned to you last year has done four drawings for me which (if they arrive safe in England) will be the admiration of the whole town & put all our English artists, even the great Mr Smith [John 'Warwick' Smith] to the blush: I flatter myself he will add much to my improvement, for he has not only taught me the management of his colours, but shewd me a very easy method of engraving drawings in the brown tints';[9] and in a notebook he recorded a careful description of Ducros' palette and the combination of colours he used. His admiration for Ducros' work continued after his return to England in 1791 and survived the artist's enforced absence from Rome between 1793 and 1808, an exile occasioned chiefly by anti-French feeling in the city, but also (according to rumours reported by Swiss residents in Rome) because of jealousy among Italian artists who resented his success and accused him of sharp practice and immoral conduct. Colt Hoare was later to attribute his detractors' jealousy to Ducros' 'superior merits'. Only one letter from the artist to his patron is known, written from Malta in 1800, in which he solicited help in finding subscribers to a series of views: 'c'est un sujet national . . . Malthe Minorque et Giberaltar sont les Boulevards [i.e. bulwarks] de la Puissance Britanique'.[10] Although nothing seems to have come of this appeal, Colt Hoare's esteem for Ducros was unabated, and found its fullest expression in the first volume of his *History of Modern Wiltshire*, 1822. It was in this carefully researched county history, chiefly important for its antiquarian information, that Colt Hoare, somewhat unexpectedly, gave a description of the collections at Stourhead, which concludes with an excursus on Ducros' water-colours. He noted the 'rapid improvement in water-colour drawing [which] has taken place within my own memory; for during my younger days, Paul Sandby was the monarch of the plain, and esteemed the best artist in this line. The next marked improvement in colouring was recognized in the drawings of Mr John Smith, now living: . . . but the advancement from *drawing* to *painting* in water-colours did not take place till after the introduction into England of the drawings of Louis du Cros . . . his works proved the force as well as the consequence, that could be given to the unsubstantial body of water-colours, and to him I attribute the first knowledge and power of water-colours. Hence have sprung a numerous succession of Artists in this line.'[11]

How far does Colt Hoare's claim stand up to examination? That a change of the kind he described took place at the end of the eighteenth century is beyond dispute. W H Pyne, an art-critic and journalist as well as an artist, writing in 1824, only two years after Colt Hoare's publication, saw the matter somewhat differently. He ascribed the change to 'Those two aspiring geniuses [Girtin and Turner] . . . developing new properties in the material with which they wrought their elegant imitations of nature, and raising the practice of watercolours, which had hitherto procured no higher title for the best works of its professors, than tinted drawings, to the rank and character of painting in watercolours. Thus these two distinguished artists, improving rapidly . . . achieved the honour of founding that English school . . . the admiration of all nations'.[12] As Pyne and Colt Hoare recognized, in their own different ways, water-colour artists were the *avant garde*, for it could be argued that landscape painting was to become the most innovative and characteristic art form of the nineteenth century. With the foundation of the Society of Painters in Water-Colour in 1804, the exponents of the medium became the first organized group to champion landscape and to mount exhibitions devoted almost exclusively to it, and to develop a technique and style that set out to rival the effect of oil-paintings. By revivifying the old topographical tradition and combining it with recent aesthetic theories they were producing some of the most advanced works of art to be seen in England at the time. Colt Hoare's explanation of the development of English water-colour painting by attributing it almost entirely to the example of Ducros reflects a somewhat exaggerated personal bias; no works by Ducros had been publicly exhibited in England and few artists could have had access to privately owned examples.

Colt Hoare was, however, not the only person to associate the increasing status of water-colour with the example of Ducros. Joseph Farington noted in his diary for 14th March 1806: 'At the Royal Society club yesterday Mr Simmonds mentioned Craig's lecture at the Royal Institution & Mr Parsons expressed his approbation of it, being with Craig, of the opinion that Water Colour painting is superior to oil painting. He formed that opinion on seeing Du Cros' drawings in Italy & the exhibition in Brook Street last year'.[13] (The reference is to the inaugural exhibition of the Society of Painters in Water-Colour). Both Colt Hoare and the unidentified Mr Parsons seem to have been impressed by the type of water-colour that in grandeur of effect and degree of finish could compete with oil-paintings. This taste was shared by most contemporary collectors and patrons. The private, intimate sketch made directly from nature, which we now particularly value and consider to be the most significant part of the British water-colour tradition, was of little interest to such connoisseurs. Ducros' patrons, particularly the British, were attracted by his depiction of recognizable places on an impressively large scale, and by the way in which he enlivened the topographical subject matter with dramatic atmospheric effects.

A more recent claim for the influence of Ducros on British art was made in 1917 by C F Bell, who suggested that an important factor in the development of water-colour lay in the contact which various British artists working in Rome in the 1770s and 1780s might have had with Swiss artists—including Ducros.[14] This hypothesis seemed to him to be confirmed by the reference to Ducros' work in *The History of Modern Wiltshire*, unknown to him in 1917 but discussed at some length in 1935 in the introduction to his catalogue of *The Drawings and Sketches of John Robert Cozens*.[15] Bell invoked Colt Hoare's discussion of Ducros' work to explain Cozens' stylistic development, suggesting that it was under 'the robust and sympathetic' influence of Ducros that 'Cozens began to experiment' while in Rome between 1776 and 1779. But this hypothesis is less convincing in the light of our fuller knowledge of the circumstances of Ducros' life. Bell believed that he had gone to Rome in about 1770 and was well established there by 1776, but it has subsequently been shown that he did not arrive until the end of 1776, that is, at about the same time as Cozens. The drawings made during Ducros' expedition to the Kingdom of the Two Sicilies and Malta in 1778 (see cat nos 51–3), which, though interesting as records of the journey are very unlike his mature work, provide no evidence that by 1779 he had developed a style that could have influenced Cozens. It was not until 1783–84—that is, after Cozens' second and last visit to Italy in 1782–83—that Ducros, doubtless encouraged by the success of his coloured etchings, began to paint the large-scale water-colours that were to find such favour with British patrons. It is perhaps of some significance that while Ducros' German contemporary Philipp Hackert is mentioned several times in the *Memoirs* of Thomas Jones (albeit rather acidly), and his influential status in Roman art circles acknowledged, Ducros is not referred to at all. This is partly because Jones, who lived in Italy from 1776 to 1783, moved to Naples in 1780 and was thus less aware of what was going on in Rome: nevertheless, the absence of any reference to Ducros in Jones' *Memoirs* tends to confirm the probability that it was not until circa 1783–84 that his reputation became established both with patrons and with his fellow artists, and casts further doubt on Bell's notion that his work was a formative influence on Cozens. There could indeed be a case for inverting Bell's argument and suggesting that the reciprocal influence between Ducros and British artists in Rome may have been partly in the opposite direction. Could Ducros have seen Cozens' sombre though richly toned and atmospheric views of the Roman Campagna (a number of which he painted in the course of his first visit to Italy) and John 'Warwick' Smith's large water-colours of Rome, painted between 1776 and 1781? Such discussions of influences are apt to be too cut and dried; it would be safer simply to observe that the artistic milieu of Rome in the 1770s and 1780s was one in which aspiring artists were quick to seize on new ideas.

An artist on whom Ducros' work does seem, however, to have had some influence was Turner, whose most important single patron in the late 1790s was Colt Hoare (they seem to have met circa 1795):[16] in July 1799 Turner told Farington that he had sixty drawings ordered, and to judge from notes in various sketchbooks, twenty-seven had been commissioned by Colt Hoare, although only some half-dozen had by that date been completed. The most important water-colours that he was asked to paint for Colt Hoare were two sets, each of ten subjects, the first depicting various buildings in and around Salisbury, the second devoted to views of the cathedral. Turner was engaged spasmodically on these projects between about 1795 and 1805, and although in the event he seems to have failed to complete the commission, the Salisbury Cathedral interiors (several of which he exhibited at the Royal Academy), executed on a very grand scale, were the most impressive and ambitious water-colours he had hitherto painted. It was these very water-colours that Colt Hoare was to single out in his discussion of Ducros' works and their influence on the English school: '. . . designs in water-colours . . . have made, within these few years past, a most astonishing progress and in many instances may be said to have attained the acme of perfection; for I question if the series of architectural drawings of Salisbury, in this apartment, executed by Mr Turner . . . will ever be surpassed.'[17] It seems altogether likely that Turner was considerably impressed by Colt Hoare's collection of Ducros' water-colours at Stourhead, and that he found in them a monumentality and dramatic atmosphere that exactly coincided with his developing taste for sublime subjects and his interest in a wide range of earlier artists: the combination, at Stourhead, of works by Ducros, an extensive collection of Piranesi's prints, and the passionate classical interests of Colt Hoare were to stimulate Turner's development at a critical moment in his career.

Hitherto, the character of Turner's water-colours had been chiefly topographical and picturesque. But by 1800 he was able to deal confidently with a much wider range of subject and of mood. It would be an exaggeration to attribute this development solely to the influence of Ducros, yet that influence should not be discounted. Even allowing for Colt Hoare's understandable bias, it seems more than likely that a mind as receptive and alert as Turner's was to the potentialities of water-colour as a medium not only for the sketch made direct from nature—for that was a lesson he had absorbed a good deal earlier— but as a vehicle for grandeur and force of effect, would have recognized in Ducros' work both an inspiration and an implied challenge. Turner's lifelong fascination with the technical aspects of his art would have been stimulated by studying Ducros' complex mixtures of water-colour, gouache and oil, his use of cut-out figures superimposed on his landscapes, and his sombre but expressive palette. Nor may the period of Turner's early association with Colt Hoare have been the end of Ducros' influence on him. An echo, albeit a faint one, of Ducros' repertoire of motifs and proto-Romantic sense of atmosphere is perhaps to be discerned in some of the colour studies made during his first visit to Rome in 1819; although at the same time it must be said that not the least remarkable quality of Turner's Roman water-colours lies in the extent to which he was able to put aside his knowledge of earlier artists' interpretations of the city.

This essay has been concerned almost wholly with the patronage of Richard Colt Hoare, who though certainly Ducros' most important British patron was not his only one. Studies of patronage are inevitably dependent on the documentation available, and the lack of such information may give a distorted impression of the relative importance of patrons. In the case of Ducros, few details about his other British patrons are known, apart from their names and occasional references in correspondence. In the case of one particularly important series, the six large water-colours painted for Sir John Acton in Naples in 1794,[18] we can only assume that the artist was helped to secure the commission by Sir William Hamilton, whom he had first met in 1778. In some cases even the works are lost. Particularly regrettable is the disappearance of an apparently unique example of a *paysage historique* by Ducros—an oil-painting of a subject taken from classical literature, *Cicero discovering the Tomb of Archimedes*—painted for the 4th Earl of Bristol —the 'Earl Bishop'—in 1784–85.[19] A Swiss compatriot saw the painting in progress, but it is not recorded in the *Catalogo della raccolta di oggetti d'arte Bristol*, published in Rome in 1804, at the time of the auction of part of the collection.

The influence of Ducros on British landscape painting was probably not on those contemporaries of his who were working in Rome in the 1770s and 1780s but, as Colt Hoare perceived, on the next generation of artists, most notably Turner, who was to become the greatest exponent of Sublime landscape painting.

1   BCU, Fonds PELIS Is 4350, fol 32 ; see *Chronology* for 1787.
2   J. G. Meusel (ed), *Miscellaneen artistischen Inhalts*, vol 9, Erfurt, 1781, p 190
3   Roland de la Platière had noted that such prints were barely worthy of mention : 'Nulle part on ne grave autant qu'à Rome, mais rien aujourd'hui qui mérite qu'on en fasse mention. On trouve bien à la Calcografia les gravures de toutes les galeries de Rome, de ses antiquités, de ses ruines, etc., mais ce ne sont que des retouches : on s'est ingéré de ses enluminer, ce qui les a portées à des prix excessifs. Les Anglais en sont fous, mais elles ne conviennent ainsi qu'à eux' (*Lettres écrites de Suisse, d'Italie, de Sicile et de Malthe en 1776, 1777, et 1778*, vol 5, Amsterdam, 1780, p 97).
4   See Brinsley Ford, 'James Byres ; Principal Antiquarian for the English Visitors to Rome', *Apollo*, XCIX (1974), pp 446–461.
5   'The Memoirs of Thomas Jones', ed. A P Oppé, *The Walpole Society*, XXXIII (1946–48), p 94.
6   Brinsley Ford, 'William Constable ; An Enlightened Yorkshire Patron', *Apollo*, XCIX (1974), p 414.
7   Colt Hoare to Hugh Hoare, 19th March 1786, in Kenneth Woodbridge, *Landscape and Antiquity : Aspects of English Culture at Stourhead 1718–1838*; 1970, p 91.
8   The most thorough account of Richard Colt Hoare's life, with particular emphasis on his patronage of contemporary artists and his archaeological interests, is to be found in Woodbridge, op cit.
9   Ibid, p 96.
10   See Appendix 1, where Ducros' letter to Colt Hoare is given in full.
11   Richard Colt Hoare, *The History of Modern Wiltshire*, Vol. I, 1822, p 82.
12   W H Pyne, *Somerset House Gazette*, I, 1824, p 66.

13   *The Diary of Joseph Farington*, ed. Kathryn Cave, Vol. VII (January 1805–June 1806), 1982, p 2691.
14   C F Bell, 'British water-colour painters: James Moore Collection', *The Walpole Society*, V (1915–17), pp 56–7.
15   C F Bell and T Girtin, 'J R Cozens: Drawings and sketches', *The Walpole Society*, XXIII (1934–35). Luke Herrmann, *Landscape Painting in Britain*, 1973, pp 80–82, discussed Bell's theory but was unconvinced of Ducros' influence on Cozens. However, he did not consider Colt Hoare's assertion that Ducros was important to Turner's development. It should be noted that Colt Hoare nowhere mentions Cozens.
16   John Gage, 'Turner and Stourhead : The Making of a Classicist?', *The Art Quarterly*, XXXVII (1974), pp 59–87. Gage suggests that Piranesi was a more powerful influence on Turner than Ducros (whose importance he however notes).
17   Richard Colt Hoare, *The History of Modern Wiltshire*, Vol. I, 1822, p 82. In the same passage, Colt Hoare also mentions Francis Nicholson (1753–1844) as one of the artists influenced by Ducros. Nicholson was commissioned circa 1813–16 by Colt Hoare to record the landscape gardens at Stourhead in a series of twenty-five elaborate water-colours (now in the British Museum). He developed a process for multiplying compositions which could conceivably have been derived from what he learnt of Ducros' methods from Colt Hoare : 'My process was by etching on a soft ground the different views of the place, from which were taken impressions with blacklead. This produced outlines so perfectly like those done by the pencil, that it was impossible to discover any difference. This was nearly half the work, and in the long days of summer I finished them at the rate of six daily'.
18   See cat nos 77–79.
19   Chessex, 1982, p 58, note 74.

Some Swiss Artists in Rome 1775–93

Luc Boissonnas

On the 8th October 1784 Jacques Louis David returned to Rome to paint *The Oath of the Horatii*, an epoch-making painting in the history of eighteenth century art. At this time three young painters who had known each other in Geneva were reunited in the Eternal City. One had trained in Geneva copying Dutch masters and had come to Rome in 1776 to make his fortune as a painter of Italian views. The second had gone at an early age to Paris to be taught at the Académie Royale des Beaux-Arts, and the third had gone to the Dresden Academy. The following brief essay examines the way in which these three men made their way in the Rome art world, where the competitive spirit was invigorating, if not wild, among artists who had come to the city from all over Europe to study the Grand Style and, if possible, make their fortunes.

The Genevan painter Pierre-Louis de la Rive left Dresden for Italy at the end of September 1784. In a letter to his wife he described crossing the frontier between Saxony and Bohemia in the middle of the night. The official, smelling 'most frightfully of liquor' was most uncivil, making him unpack all his baggage: 'This kept me three dreadful hours, and fortunately he did not find my sealed letters'[1] These were the letters of recommendation which no eighteenth century traveller would have been without, since they provided the social and professional links which could establish a traveller in other countries. Once a useful letter was obtained, judicious use of it could give rise to others. In another letter to his wife a few weeks later De la Rive spoke of the cordiality of the Italians he met: 'They put their minds to solving anything that could give you trouble, they genuinely take care of you, trying to obtain useful or pleasant recommendations for you. When I arrived in Ferrara at the home of Count Pepoli,[2] a young man of 26, his first action was to give me a letter for the Venetian ambassador in Rome, I already had one in fact [from Mme Corner] for Count Marulli, ambassador to the Grand Duke of Tuscany; Mme Corner[3] had forgotten that one, I accepted it and he gave it to me open, containing all the enthusiasm Mme Corner had put in hers. . . . I only mention this to you to prove the difference. In Dresden nobody would give me a note for the Agdallo family, which would give a fine foothold in Venice. With great reluctance I was promised one for the house of Hohendal at Ratisbonne when I returned, and this was considered to be doing me a great honour'[4]

Letters of recommendation were sometimes rather different. Ducros had tried to persuade De la Rive to go to Rome eight years before and had eventually gone there with Isaac-Jacob Lacroix, probably arriving at his destination in November 1776. On 20th December 1776 the publisher and art dealer Chrétien de Mechel of Basel wrote to Alexander Trippel, a sculptor from Schaffhausen, concerning 'a few of those cavaliers against whom I feel duty bound to warn you'.[5] Having said all the bad things he knew about a painter from Hanover named 'Diz',[6] Mechel continued: 'At present in Rome there is, or should be, a certain Lacroix of Morat, an engraver and former student of mine, who treacherously ran away from his apprenticeship and engaged in other wicked pranks; both gentlemen are windbags, and if they carry on in this way they will come to a bad end. But do tell us where they are and what they are doing'. Trippel, who had come to Rome two months earlier with Mechel's help, replied virtually by return of mail on 22nd January 1777 (letters between Switzerland and Rome taking some four to five weeks): 'Lacroix and his friend visited me on their arrival, but they have not been here since, my reception being none too cordial. They are lodging not far away and I can see into their rooms. As far as I can see, they live well and entertain now and then; the engraver is to do one of Herr Hackert's landscapes, the birthplace of the present Pope . . .'[7]

How did Ducros of Yverdon and Lacroix of Payerne meet each other? Was it at Yverdon where Ducros' father was a drawing master? It has been suggested that they met at Mechel's studio, but if they *had* worked together before going to Rome then it would probably have been in Balthasar Dunker's studio in Bern.[8] Lacroix had left Mechel's studio some years before and completed his training in Bern with Dunker and Eichler.[9]

Dunker himself worked at Mechel's studio from August 1772 to the spring of the following year; he had originally studied under Jakob-Philip Hackert, whom he accompanied to Paris, and then under Wille. Dunker came from Stralsund, and moved to Bern to join his friends Sigmund Freudenberger and J L Aberli who had also studied under Wille. Mechel may have had a low opinion of Lacroix, but it seems that Dunker got on very well with the young artist from the Vaud, perhaps even encouraging him to leave the disagreeable Mechel, who exploited the young artists in his service and rarely allowed them to sign plates engraved in his studio. In Dunker, Lacroix found a more generous employer and in the French edition of 1775 of Haller's German poetry the frontispiece was drawn and engraved by Dunker and finished off by Lacroix.[10]

The comment in Trippel's letter to Mechel of how 'the engraver plans on doing one of Herr Hackert's landscapes, the birthplace of the present Pope' refers to the *View of Cesena* (fig. 6). This is mentioned in Meusel's *Miscellaneen artistischen Inhalts* (1782) as 'painted by Jaq. Phil. Hackert and engraved by Lacroix'. J H Fuseli's edition of Pilkington's *Dictionary of Painters* (1806) called it one of Hackert's best paintings. It was no mere chance that the young engraver was given this commission so soon after his arrival in Rome, but rather the result of the recommendation Dunker must have given him for his former teacher and friend Hackert. Paired with this engraving was a *View of St. Peter's, Rome* 'seen from the Ponte Molle', also painted by Hackert, and, according to the *Dictionary*, etched by Dunker, engraved by Lacroix and finished by Volpato.

Dunker gave Lacroix and Ducros the best possible entrée into Roman artistic circles. De la Rive's Dresden friends had recommended him to Councillor Reifenstein, the official supplier of works of art and antiquities to the courts of Dresden and St. Petersburg, who in turn introduced De la Rive into the famous and formidable coterie of Angelica Kauffmann. In November 1784 he wrote to his wife: 'I have met the famous Angelika Kauffmann. I have fallen into the midst of this whole clique of charlatans, but although I get on well enough with all of them, I could not think less of them *in petto*. Artists keen to be accepted here are obliged to court the favours of Hackert, Reifenstein and Angelika, otherwise there are no recommendations to the foreigners who all end up there. Ducros has got on their wrong side through his avoidance of everything that aims to impress, and he is in trouble'[11]. However, at the beginning of his time in Rome Ducros must have been in favour with this circle of artists. He achieved an entrée with ease because he had come from Switzerland with Lacroix, and had worked with Dunker and Aberli in Bern.

fig. 6
Lacroix after Hackert,
Veduta della città di Cesena,
Kupferstichkabinet der ETH, Zurich, 1776.

The latter led to his mastery of line-etching, the 'manière Aberli', which Ducros is traditionally said to have introduced into Italy around 1779 when he began to publish the *Vues de Rome* with Volpato. A skilled printer with a large studio, Volpato would not have entrusted Ducros with etching plates for which he, as publisher, took financial responsibility, had he not had full confidence in the Swiss artist.

Two years after his arrival in Rome, Lacroix returned to Switzerland for health reasons and worked for booksellers, engraving plates for illustrated works. Carl Brun's *Schweizerisches Künstler-Lexikon* (1905) mentions a Jean Lacroix who engraved plates for a book by Charles Bonnet, and an Isaac-Jacob Lacroix who went to Rome with Ducros. Brun gives no precise information on the former, but he may be the same person as Isaac-Jacob,[12] who would have been warmly recommended to Charles Bonnet whom Ducros regarded as his patron and life-long friend. A print entitled *Première vue des Environs du Lac Léman du côté du midi* (fig. 7) appeared in 1780, drawn and etched by S Malgo, a Danish painter, and engraved by I Lacroix. In 1781 the two artists collaborated on a second version, dedicated to Charles Bonnet. Lacroix also engraved the plates after drawings by Henri Ploetz for the *Mémoire sur . . . la Salamandre*, in volumes X and XI of Charles Bonnet's natural histories, published in 1781 at Neuchâtel. In his letters to Bonnet, Ducros speaks of Ploetz in the warmest of terms.

For Jean-Pierre Saint-Ours[13], who won the Grand Prix for painting in 1780, the introduction to Rome's artistic circles came through the French Academy in Rome. Being Swiss, he was not eligible for the royal allowance that went with his prize and had to pay for his own trip. Immediately upon arriving he visited his honoured teacher Vien, Director of the Academy, which was then in the Via del Corso. Delighted as Vien was to see him, he could only offer Saint-Ours a place as an external student at the Palazzo Mancini, as was an occasional practice. But for room and board, Saint-Ours was treated with all the respect due to a winner of the Grand Prix. Vien wrote to the Comte d'Angivilliers about the young man: 'Master Saint-Ours, my former pupil, who has earned the first prize medal for painting, arrived yesterday in Rome; he intends to study well, and if his talents match his ambition, he will return to Paris and neglect no way of paying you homage; he has enough sense to realise that the place of his birth excluded him from the number of His Majesty's stipendiaries . . .'[14]

Saint-Ours first lodged in an inn near SS. Trinità dei Monti in the Via Sistina, then called the Strada Felice, where he shared rooms with the painter Gugliermo Papi.[15] The sculptor Giuseppe Sodi lived in the neighbouring apartments. In 1782 he moved in with his young cousin and pupil, Constant Vaucher, then fourteen years old, in the Via Margutta at the foot of the Pinciò hill. They stayed at the house 'Al Mosaico detta delli focchetti'[16] until 1785, and in 1783 were joined by Jacques Sablet who had shared apartments with Ducros in the Via della Croce the previous year. Like Saint-Ours, Sablet was a pupil of Vien, and had come with him to Rome in 1775 following his teacher's appointment as Director of

fig. 7
Lacroix after Malgo, *Première vue des environs du Lac Léman du côté du midi*, 1780. Private Collection.

the Academy.[17] Both men had worked under Vien for four years in Paris. Saint-Ours wrote in his autobiography: 'I loved this gentle, solitary and studious life, and after working for two years I was required to exhibit alongside my fellow students at the Academy'.[18]

This exhibition took place every year on St Louis' day, and the presence of Cardinal de Bernis, French Ambassador to Rome attracted the city's high society.[19] This was a real opportunity for young Frenchmen to meet connoisseurs who could often be relied upon for a commission. Lagrenée, Vien's successor as Director at the Palazzo Mancini, reported on the success of this exhibition to the Comte d'Angivilliers: 'Saint-Ours, a prize-winner, but not a member of the Academy, distinguished himself with two excellent life-size nudes and a sketch of the Olympic Games, the virile composition of which makes one regret that he was not born a Frenchman.[20]

As a result of Saint-Ours' success at the exhibition Lagrenée took the liberty of asking d'Angivilliers if he wanted Saint-Ours 'to send him some of his works with the others in order to obtain the opinions and advice of the Academy, whose adopted son he is'.[21] After consultation with Pierre, Director of the Academy in Paris, d'Angivilliers wrote back to Lagrenée, making it clear that Saint-Ours was regarded with some favour: "I have . . . heard . . . about the success of the exhibition of the stipendiaries' work which opened on St. Louis' day. All I will say to you on this matter is since Master Saint-Ours is not a stipendiary, his works should not have been there. I am, however, delighted to learn that he is so promising. You may send his two nudes[22] with those of the stipendiaries. Mr Pierre, who is interested in this young artist, has agreed to pass on to him the opinions he will require'.[23]

Lagrenée learned his lesson and refrained from mentioning Saint-Ours' presence in the Palazzo Mancini exhibitions and the young painter continued to show his paintings alongside those of his fellow students at the Academy. The second time he did so was at the end of the same year in an exhibition in honour of the Duc de Chartres who was passing through Rome. His work was next seen at the St. Louis' day exhibition in 1783. At these exhibitions Saint-Ours had the opportunity of showing the public the preparatory sketches and studies for the three works which were to make his name as an historical painter: *The Olympic Games*,[24] *The Choice of the Children of Sparta*[25] and *The German Marriages*.[26]

Pierre-Louis de la Rive only came to Rome for a year and did not need to earn a living. He obtained an entrée into Roman life with the greatest of ease: 'I was received by Ducros and Saint-Ours, my two old friends, with the greatest cordiality. Both of them devoted the whole of yesterday to me, taking me on walks round all the antique sites. My emotion at each step we took was of great amusement to them'.[27] They introduced him to several landscape painters, including the Frenchman Boguet-Didier (whose portrait Saint-Ours painted in 1787) Jacques Sablet and his friend Simon Denis d'Anvers, Saint-Ours' neighbour in the Via del Babuino. But competition between established artists in Rome was so great that De la Rive had to take precautions: 'To prevent artists turning against me and in order to see them freely here I have presented myself as a simple amateur and have behaved accordingly; as long as I am here I must keep up the same tone.'[28] Such caution may seem excessive, but one has only to remember how artists like David, then painting his *Horatii*, were at pains to prevent colleagues from entering their studios, and at most allowed visits only from those patrons they dared not alienate for fear of losing business. 'If I produced something here,' said De la Rive, 'I would have a thousand hounds baying at my heels, some loudly, others quietly, trying to bite me in the back'.[29] Although competition among artists did breed mistrust, one could not take as a general rule Béat de Hennezel's description of the Roman water-colourists and *vedutisti* as 'crimson with pride, jealousy and impertinence' tearing each other to shreds after praising themselves to excess in the presence of a visitor.[30]

Saint-Ours fell gravely ill in 1791 while drawing with his friends in the Castelli Romani. He wrote in his autobiography how his friends, seeing him close to death, elicited the help of a skilled doctor from Montpellier who was the brother of the painter and royal stipendiary Fabre and put him on the road to recovery in five or six days: 'If I had died, I would have suffered little . . . but I was very much aware of the friendship, the concern of my colleagues, friends and all my acquaintances'.[31] Nearly twenty years later Ducros, having just learned of Saint-Ours' death, wrote to De la Rive: 'My dear friend, like you

I have just been afflicted by the cruel loss we have suffered of our mutual friend, the late Monsieur Saint-Ours; Geneva did not know this great man who should have had a good pension and been educating pupils worthy of him'. He concluded: 'We are far apart, but I often think of you and the golden age of our picturesque travels in Savoy and Rome'.[32]

1   Letter from P-L de la Rive to his wife, Prague, 30 September 1784. MS fr 2397, BPU Geneva.
2   Allesandro-Ercole Comte Pepoli, Italian writer (Venice 1757—Florence 1796).
3   Cécile Corner (née Grimani), sister of Marina Pepoli-Grimani, mother of Comte Pepoli.
4   Letter from De la Rive to his wife, Bologna, 2 November 1784.
5   Alexander Trippel, Briefwechsel Kunstgesellschaft, Zürich, M29 Musée des Beaux-Arts, Zurich.
6   Albert Christoph Dies (Hanover 1755—Vienna 1822) worked for several months with Mechel in Basle, arrived in Rome 24 August 1775; worked with Piranesi, then with Volpato and Ducros. Aloïs Hirt, 1787; F Noack, Thieme-Becker, IX, 1913.
7   Letter from Alexander Trippel to Mechel 22 January 1777. Working from a rough copy of this lost letter, L H Wüthrich in *Christian von Mechel* (Basle, 1956) p 63 transcribes *Camoci* for *Camar [a]d* (elsewhere Trippel wrote *orgenal* for *original*) who he identifies as one of Lacroix's assistants. This could only refer to Ducros, with whom Lacroix stayed after he came to Rome. See Chessex, 1982, p 44.
8   Balthasar Anton Dunker (Stralsund 1746—Bern 1807).
9   Gottfried Matthias Eichler (Erlangen 1748—Augsburg after 1818).
10   *Poésies de Monsieur Haller* (translated from German by Tscharner). Revised edition, Bern, Société typographique, 1775. Frontispiece drawn and etched by Dunker, and engraved by Lacroix. See F C Lonchamp *Manuel du bibliophile Suisse 1475—1914*, p1371.
11   Letter from Rome, 26 November 1788.
12   This opinion is shared by L H Wüthrich, op cit, p 62, note 18. According to Pierre Chessex the Fonds H B de Saussure (BPU, Geneva) contains a letter by I J Lacroix dated Morat 10 October 1779 which indicates that he returned from Rome and was looking for work in Geneva from this date.
13   (Geneva 4 April 1752—Geneva 6 April 1809).
14   Vien to d'Angivilliers from Rome, 10 January 1781, Corr Dir XIV/78 no 8094.
15   AV, S Andrea delle Fratte, 1781, vol 145 fol 27 v.
16   AV, Santa Maria del Popolo, 1782, fol 42.
17   See Nantes, Lausanne, Rome, 1985, p 25 ff.
18   MS no 1939/141 Beaux-Arts, Musée d'Art et d'Histoire, Geneva.
19   Francois-Joachim de Pierre de Bernis (1715–94), Cardinal and French minister in Rome from 1769.
20   Corr Dir XIV/251, no 8275, Rome, 28 August 1782.
21   Ibid.
22   *Académie de femme*, Société des Arts, Geneva. *Académie d'homme*, Musée de Mulhouse.
23   D'Angivilliers to Lagrenée. Corr Dir XIV/267, no 8298, 30 September 1782.
24   Musée d'Art et d'Histoire, Geneva.
25   Ibid.
26   Bayerische Staatsgemäldesammlungen, Munich.
27   De la Rive to his wife, 22 November 1784, MS fr 2397, BPU Geneva
28   Ibid. 12 August 1785.
29   Ibid. 3 February 1785.
30   Journal of Béat de Hennezel, ACV bt 51. Partly published by Gilliard, 1914.
31   Autobiography, MS no 1939/141, Beaux-Arts, Musée d'Art et d'Histoire, Geneva.
32   Letter from Ducros to De la Rive, Lausanne 17 May 1809, BPU MS fr 2399.

The Museo Pio-Clementino in Rome and the views by Ducros and Volpato

Francis Haskell

From the very first years of the sixteenth century the most famous works of art in the world were kept in a courtyard attached to a villa (the Villa del Belvedere—so called because it had been raised on a hill) within the complex of gardens and courts and corridors and other buildings that made up the Pope's palace in the Vatican. Artists and visitors from all over Europe came there to copy and study and rhapsodise over the *Apollo*, the *Laocoon*, the *Antinous*, the *Torso* and a few other antique statues which became familiar to everyone with any claim to education through the innumerable reproductions in every medium that were made of them. But, rather surprisingly, we have almost no satisfactory visual record of how these sculptures were actually displayed. Even written accounts are not as full as might be expected, although it is certain that the principal sculptures had been placed in decorated niches fitted into the walls of the courtyard and that in those niches they had been partly concealed by shutters which (in the interests of prudery) had been inserted in the middle of the sixteenth century: some of the other statues had been mounted as fountains and the general effect was probably that of a formal garden. A few, but not many, changes were made to this overall pattern during the next two hundred years.

As from 1771, however, this whole arrangement was radically transformed, and—in a move whose enlightenment and intelligence will surely seem totally incomprehensible to governments of the later twentieth century—an impoverished papacy responded to a crisis affecting the heritage of Rome not with neglect or vandalism but with imagination and enterprise. The crisis had been caused by two factors. Excavations were bringing to light a vast number of antique statues for which no space was available (the twin palaces on the Capitol were already full) and extravagantly rich (and often unscrupulous) collectors and dealers from foreign countries were trying to remove whatever they could lay their hands on. It was in these circumstances that Pope Clement XIV (1769–74) found time, amid the pressures on him to suppress the Jesuits, to inaugurate a great new museum in the Vatican—an enterprise that was continued with even greater vigour after his death by Pope Pius VI (1775–99) who, as papal treasurer, had always been the leading spirit behind it. The building of the Museo Pio-Clementino (and the later galleries attached to it) brings to a fitting and spectacular end some three centuries of papal patronage in Rome for it is in its own way as splendid an achievement as any of the more familiar monuments of the Renaissance and Baroque periods. And the views produced by Ducros, a few of which are to be seen in the present exhibition (cat nos 57–62, figs 8–10), give us a remarkable indication of what had been carried out over a period of some twenty years. They also have a particular poignancy because they had hardly been published before many of the famous statues shown in them had been seized by invading French armies. After the downfall of Napoleon, however, most of the looted art returned to Rome, and the Museo Pio-Clementino still today looks essentially as we see it in these etchings—a unique case of survival among the great museums of the world.

The construction of the museum took place in two principal stages which correspond approximately to the reigns of the two Popes who promoted it. At first the architects (Alessandro Dori, followed by Michelangelo Simonetti) were primarily concerned to adapt existing structures for the display of antiquities and to fit new rooms and galleries into the somewhat awkward spaces available. This meant that in its initial period much of the new museum remained somewhat similar in character to the galleries of Roman palaces as they had developed during the sixteenth and seventeenth centuries: sometimes the original decoration was retained, and sometimes it was imitated in the new rooms added to the initial buildings. Ducros' plate of the *Sala dei Busti* shows this aspect of the museum very clearly (cat no 62). But by far the most decisive activity carried out during the pontificate of Clement XIV was the total transformation of the original sculpture court itself. The rather casual arrangement which had prevailed until now was replaced by a regular porticoed loggia, rather dry in style, and it was probably at this time that a number of bas-reliefs were inserted into the structure so that the very celebrated sculptures which

fig. 8
Volpato and Ducros,
*Cortile del Belvedere
con Apollo*,
Pfaueninsel, Berlin.

still remained in the octagon courtyard were no longer as isolated as they had once been: this was a change that distressed some visitors who complained that a surfeit of decoration distracted their concentration on the statues themselves. Unfortunately Ducros' illustrations which were made after the final transformation of the whole complex of galleries do not enable us to be certain exactly when individual changes were carried out; nor do they let us know the various 'promotions' and 'demotions' of the most admired statues at a time when there was evidently some hesitation as to exactly which ones should be fitted into the places of honour.

The completion of the museum under Pius VI involved far more drastic action than had

fig. 9
Volpato and Ducros,
*Galleria delle statue con
Cleopatra*,
Pfaueninsel, Berlin.

fig. 10
Volpato and Ducros,
*Cortile del Belvedere
con Laocoonte*,
Pfaueninsel, Berlin.

been taken under his predecessor. In particular it led to the ruthless destruction of the chapel of the Villa del Belvedere, which had been extensively frescoed by Mantegna—this was particularly ironical (not to say tragic) in view of the fact that it was in these very years that Mantegna was winning back the great reputation which he had once enjoyed and also because Mantegna had been the earliest proponent of the many attempts subsequently made to reconstruct the lost world of antiquity—of which the Museo Pio-Clementino itself provided one of the most ambitious examples.

Indeed this second stage in the creation of the museum offered the papal architect (Simonetti and later Giuseppe Camponese) and his team of decorators a far freer hand than they had enjoyed until now, and they certainly took advantage of this to try and give the visitor some impression of the Rome which so haunted their imaginations—partly because it had given birth to those very works of art which they were engaged in accommodating. Yet (as happened elsewhere in Rome during the last decades of the eighteenth century) an extreme monumentality of architectural effect was often combined with a very lavish scheme of pictorial adornment, and it seems that this richness did not have a universal appeal: certainly the prints of Ducros and some other artists convey an impression of austerity which is at times somewhat misleading.

Extraordinarily little documentation has (yet) come to light about the principles which underlay the organisation of the new museum, but it is almost certain that they must have been devised by the papal antiquaries Giovanni Battista Visconti (1722–84) and his far more brilliant son Ennio Quirino Visconti (1751–1818). Ennio Quirino was the greatest connoisseur and scholar of the age, and he was later to create the antique galleries of the Musée Napoléon in Paris which (as a result of French expropriations from the papal states) were to include some of the most famous pieces for whose installation he had been responsible in Rome. Rather surprisingly perhaps, the basis for his arrangement of the sculptures was thematic rather than historical, and in this it recalled the work of older antiquarians of a previous generation rather than that of his mentor, Winckelmann, who had introduced the notion of continuous chronological development into the study of ancient art. Sometimes this concentration on subject matter strikes us—and must surely have struck some of his contemporaries—as almost comically pedantic. Thus the *Meleager*—one of the most admired of all antique statues—was placed in the Sala degli Animali, along with assorted (and heavily restored) dogs, birds and crocodiles, presumably because attached to the figure of the nude youth (the proportions of whose body were often compared to those of the *Antinous*, that very model of perfection) were to be seen his hunting dog and the decapitated head of a wild boar.

But, above all, it was the dramatic impact made by the museum that was emphasised by Visconti and his designers. It is true that lack of available space meant that there was no opportunity of building an imposing façade, but once inside the Museo Pio-Clementino the visitor was drawn down long, imposing galleries, lined with standing figures, to carefully contrived climaxes at each end which clearly reflected the lessons derived from glowing altarpieces in Baroque churches; circular rooms and domed halls, corridors, recesses, vestibules and cunningly illuminated staircases all contribute to an unforgettable effect, even though so many of the sculptures actually to be seen in the museum may have lost much of their appeal. We can never forget that this is the century of Piranesi; and in this respect the Museo Pio-Clementino had no true successors, even though so many of its individual features were to be imitated in sculpture galleries all over the world.

Many visitors were deeply moved by this evocative combination of drama and clear display. The English (Catholic) archaeologist John Chetwode Eustace put the case most eloquently: 'It consists of several apartments, galleries, halls, and temples, some lined with marble, others paved with ancient mosaics, and all filled with statues, vases, candelabra, tombs, and altars. The size and proportion of these apartments, their rich materials and furniture, the well managed light poured in upon them, and the multiplicity of admirable articles collected in them and disposed in the most judicious and striking arrangement, fill the mind of the spectator with astonishment and delight, and form the most magnificent and grand combination that perhaps has ever been beheld or can almost be imagined. Never were the divinities of Greece and Rome honoured with nobler temples; never did they stand on richer pedestals; never were more glorious domes spread over their heads; or brighter pavements extended at their feet. Seated each in a shrine of bronze or marble, they seemed to look down on a crowd of votaries and once more to challenge the homage of mankind; while kings and emperors, heroes and philosophers, drawn up in ranks before or around them, increased their state and formed a majestic and becoming retinue'.

Not everyone shared this enthusiasm. Some visitors to the museum seem to have felt that an excess of (often indifferent) objects diluted the quality of what had once been a small collection composed only of masterpieces; and others appear to have looked upon the dramatic style of display as inherently meretricious. It is very tempting to believe that Ducros may have had reservations of this kind—or, at least, that he may have designed his views of the museum for art-lovers who were made somewhat uneasy by such a startlingly new approach to antiquity. It so happens that we can compare his illustrations of the museum with another, similar, series which were engraved soon afterwards by Vincenzo Feoli from drawings by Tommaso Costa, Francesco Miccinelli and Feoli himself (fig 11). The information conveyed by the two sets is—as one would expect (or at least hope)—very similar; but in every case Ducros gives us a more sober impression of what was to be seen in the museum: the richness, the crowding, the contrasts, the colour are invariably played down. It is notoriously difficult (not to say misleading) to attribute differences of style to differences of approach—but if we acknowledge that the creation of the Museo Pio-Clementino (which was conceived and built at a period when aesthetic controversies were unusually articulate) represents an important moment in the history of European culture, we should scrutinise with great care and respect any evidence which can throw light on contemporary attitudes to such a development. The etchings by Ducros to be seen here are thus of considerable interest and importance.

fig. 11
Feoli,
Veduta del Museo Pio-Clementino, Istituto Nazionale per la Grafica, Calcografia, Rome.

Ducros' Technical Methods

Westby Percival Prescott

Ducros developed his water-colour paintings in several well-defined stages, consisting of a preliminary drawing, an under-painting (or dead colouring), a finishing layer, and a retouching stage. This process was often completed in isolated parts of the canvas or paper with large areas left untouched so as to allow his assistants to add figures. The final retouching stage was usually made by Ducros himself, who continued to make additions or changes to his own designs.

Because he often worked in a large format uncommon to water-colour painting of the period, he was at times forced to combine several sheets of paper which would finally be pasted onto canvas. In some cases, he would even add new pieces of paper to enable further additions to be made or paste extra sheets on top of the original painting in the last stage of the work, as can be seen in his painting of the Colosseum (cat no 3). The result sometimes gives the impression of an oil painting rather than a water-colour, and Ducros in fact treated the work as such by adding thin washes of paint and glazes, using gamboge yellow (a water soluble gum) transparent brown, crimson and blue. But although these additions of intense, transparent colour and repeated glazes substantially enriched the original effect, they created specific problems of conservation which will be discussed below.

Ducros' use of colours was on the whole conventional for the period. Such colours as Vandyke brown, bistre, and occasionally sepia provided sonorous brown tones, while Prussian blue gave an intense, cool blue tonality which dominates much of his work. The employment of a more delicate, warmer blue such as the more expensive lapis lazuli, was reserved for special occasions. His flesh colours include lake, red ochre and vermillion, but sometimes he used a more unstable red lead, minium, to create accents and often to depict flames. Highlights were generally tinted in Naples yellow or yellow ochre.

Ducros' use of colours generally anticipates aspects of Goethe's ideas expressed in his *Zur Farbenlehre* (1810). Goethe described in some depth how certain specific colour properties might be used to create optical effects. The English Romantics adopted these ideas in their own works at about the same time, using scumbling and glazing, as did Ducros, to add to the substantial or fluid qualities of the scene depicted. Ducros in particular created a misty aura in his landscapes, especially in his intense representation of sky, by following these principles and by the employment of semi-transparent paint covered by a blue or pinkish blue glaze. The impression created is one of true substance and density which was greatly admired in water-colour painting in the late eighteenth century.

One of the most striking and original elements in Ducros' paintings is his use of light. His works demonstrate the different sources and forms described by Gérard de Lairesse in *Het Groot Schilderboeck* (1707), a work available in a French translation from 1787. Lairesse described several kinds of light sources which could be used separately or in combination: common light; directional light (for example, sunlight); the aurora, a central light; reflected, and frontal light. Ducros was particularly interested in exploring the so-called aurora and the frontal light. The aurora is a light source emanating from the centre that gradually spreads outwards and slowly diminishes in intensity. Frontal light, or more simply fronting, as it was sometimes called, is an additional or imaginary source from a position in front of the scene that illuminates the darkest parts of the composition. Ducros may be said to have mastered the aurora more successfully than any other water-colour artist of his day. The effect may be seen particularly in his shimmering leaves and flickering sunlight, as well as in the back-lit clouds and shafts of light that spread outward.

Examples may be cited to illustrate more clearly the ideas and techniques Ducros employed. The *Arch of Constantine* (cat no 2), for example, uses warm, frontal lighting and a pinkish tonality which permeates the shadowed areas. The distances are delineated

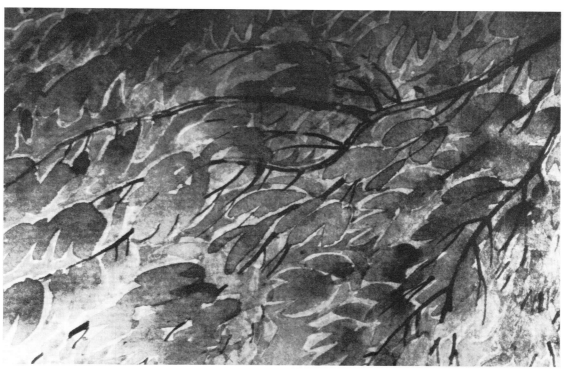

fig. 12   Ducros, *Interior of the Amphitheatre at Pozzuoli*, detail cat 32.

fig. 13   Ducros, *Virgil's Tomb*, detail cat 35.   41

by ochres in the foreground, a greenish blue and pale blue for the middle distance and background. The rich sky has a deep, substantial quality as a result of a layer of oil paint over the water-colour base. Repeated glazing, however, has darkened the effect considerably, making it difficult to distinguish the original intensity of colour and brilliance common in Ducros' work. Yet the original state of the blue sky must have resembled that in the *Interior of the Amphitheatre at Pozzuoli* (cat no 32) which can now be studied in its restored state.

In this example, the work is painted on a single sheet of paper with a central crease still visible from when the painting was executed. The work is painted mostly in water-colour, but with additions of gouache. Of particular importance here is the treatment of the foliage. These areas were originally left blank over a slight layer of yellow wash, while the shadows were painted in darker transparent yellow containing gamboge. The leaves were then drawn in a greyish brown wash of carbon black, Prussian blue or indigo and burnt siena in a medium possibly thickened by the addition of sugar. The underlying layer of yellow is never fully obliterated, creating a sparkling transparent effect of light which is augmented by a margin of exposed yellow at the edges (fig 12).

Ducros used a similar method in his *Virgil's Tomb, Posillipo* (cat no 35), but here the branches are made lighter than the leaves by the use of gouache (fig 13). In his *Storm at Night, Cefalù* (cat no 41) a far more complicated system is used. The clusters of rocks are painted in ochres, dark transparent browns and are heightened with Naples yellow. The rose highlights of the stormy sky are made with white and Naples yellow mixed with lake and other organic pigments. The opaque colours were also made into thin washes throughout the work and painted over layers of deep transparent blue or brown. These 'scumbles' were then re-glazed with further washes until a stage was reached when further highlights became necessary. This interplay between opaque and transparent layers of paint gave Ducros' works a complexity which, in many cases, exceeded that of oil painting.

The Conservation of Ducros' Water-Colours

Olivier Masson

The conservation of Ducros' works presents unusual problems. His methods of painting were often artistically original but technically unsound and as a result many types of damage have occurred. The later ambitious works made on several sheets of paper and painted in a combination of media (water-colour, resins, soluble gums and oils) are the most problematical. The surfaces are usually rubbed and the paint abraded in many places. The secondary canvas backing applied by the artist often bulges and shows tears. The paintings which have been exposed to light have suffered most. Some colours have faded while the paper has turned brown in places through oxidization (see Appendix 3).

These features are commonplace in water-colours and are disturbing, but in Ducros' works one sometimes also finds large areas of darkened varnish which leave unsightly streaks or dribbles or even completely obscure the lighter and cooler parts of the painting. Even more serious and more difficult to rectify are the layers of oil paint which at times lie below the discoloured varnish in a brittle, cracked and yellow state. The structural condition of all these layers varies in strength as does their degree of yellowing or opacity. But it becomes rapidly apparent when one examines some of the paintings that although the varnish layers may have been applied by the artist, they no longer serve their original purpose of increasing the contrast and freshening the colour and instead only partially obscure the paintings or disfigure them completely.

In works as structurally complicated as Ducros' paintings no single action of cleaning or conservation, such as the removal of darkened varnish, can be taken without artistic implications. Fortunately, the layers exhibiting the greatest deterioration and thus alteration in colour are on or near the surface and can often be treated separately and progressively. The darkness long imposed by the discoloured varnish on the cool, subtle colour of Ducros has now been reduced or removed entirely and the paintings in their restored state have regained much of their original vitality.

As more paintings in the studio collection in Lausanne were examined and experience was gained into Ducros' methods and materials, a conservation policy was arrived at: the aim of restoring the pictures to a state close to their original appearance was balanced by the desire to avoid taking any action which would alter the artistic intention in any way. It is fortunate that, although the methods Ducros used may be at fault, his intentions are clear for the most part and we can recognise the most obvious contradictions and rectify them when it is safe to do so. Where there are areas of doubt, we have endeavoured to leave the picture to speak for itself. For example, the often unsightly margins to different sheets of paper which Ducros painted rather crudely, have, in most cases, been left unretouched. There has been no interference with the drawing or replacement of loss of colour caused by the fading of organic pigments. Where it has proved possible, the discolouration caused by oxidization of the paper and painting has been reduced. The lost colour values, particularly noticeable in the intense deep blues and the dark transparent browns, has been regained by the application of a thin layer of cherry gum, a sound and traditional way of increasing depth of colour and one which safely replaces the numerous layers of spirit-based resin varnish which Ducros applied.

The old fabric (medium fine, tabby weave linen) which formed the original supports for many of Ducros' paintings was found in most cases to be weak, acidic and affected by mould. The flour paste used in the artist's studio to attach the water-colour to the canvas support was found to be too brittle in all cases. Its removal with the old fabric support allowed the transparency of the original paper to reappear and the paintings gained greatly in luminosity as a result.

The original sheets of sized, hand-made laid paper used by Ducros sometimes varied in thickness and make. They were embrittled and had many irregularities of plane. It was essential that these papers should relax evenly and obtain an equilibrium suited to all the pieces of paper forming the painting. To achieve this the paintings were placed in a sealed humidity chamber specially constructed to accommodate these large works. The period of relaxation and the percentage of relative humidity varied for each. In some cases, the presence of oil paint was a factor which had to be taken into careful consideration as too much humidity could cause cleavage of the paint. Fortunately this condition was never encountered but the value of this relaxation treatment rapidly became apparent. Planar distortion became controllable even when caused by the change of direction of laid lines in the paper.

The paintings were then placed onto a cold-air-flow suction table in a dampened relaxed state. The porous surface of the table allowed the air to circulate and gently pull the paper down and hold it flat during the period of treatment with solvents. Steam, externally applied and water (or water-ethanol mixtures) were brought into contact with the painted surface and evacuated through the table simultaneously removing the impurities. Local areas of damage were treated individually and stabilized without affecting the whole work which was maintained in an evenly held state throughout the operation. Dark irregular stains caused by oxidization of the paper or past water damage were successfully removed with repeated application of water.

Areas of discoloured oil paint, which obscured some of the skies and bore little relation to adjacent water-colour were treated with water-ethanol mixtures and other solvents. Sometimes a marked reduction of yellowing was observed after a single operation and subsequent drying. Repeated treatments with selected solvents largely removed the discolourations without affecting the stability of the paint in any way. Flaking paint rarely occurs in Ducros' work, and no weakening of the paint layers or paper was observed during these treatments.

The paintings were then backed with Japanese paper (*usumino*) to increase their strength, and later dried between sheets of felt. They were then attached to a Japanese drying screen to dry to an evenly stretched state while retaining all of their three-dimensional properties. The paintings were later given a mild fumigation treatment and made ready for relining onto a new fabric support. The lining process was carried out using a vacuum-hot table at a low pressure, with the surface protected by a layer of soft synthetic foam. Glass-fibre fabric was chosen as the most suitable material for the support, and the paintings were attached with a thermo-setting ethylene vinyl acetate resin compound made by Lascaux (based on BEVA 371).

Although the choice of glass-fibre as a backing for paper might be considered unusual, the advantages gained over any natural fibre are substantial, both in stability, moisture resistance and also resistance to the growth of micro-organisms. The presence of a layer of Japanese paper between the original drawing and the new support enables the safe removal of the glass fibre at a later stage if this ever becomes necessary. The paintings were attached to new wooden stretchers and panels forming moisture barriers were placed over the reverse providing protection from variations of climate and accidental damage.

Retouching was necessary in most cases and was carried out in water-colour in areas of obtrusive damage. Ducros' own retouchings, which in some cases are disconcertingly obvious, have not been modified in any way and every attempt has been made to preserve the historical integrity of the paintings.

We would like to acknowledge the generous help received from Mr Alois Diethelm of Lascaux Restauro, S.A. Zurich. The initial experiments using the cold air-flow table were conducted in his laboratory on a table specially constructed for the treatment of Ducros' works. Without his assistance the restoration of some of the most disfigured paintings would certainly not have been possible. The conservation work was carried out over a period of two years in the Atelier Boissonnas in Zurich by the author and Nicholas Boissonnas.

CATALOGUE

The Ducros Collection in Lausanne

After Ducros died his two brothers decided to put the whole of the painter's personal collection up for sale in order to pay off debtors and provide for the future of his son, whose guardians they were. The *Gazette de Lausanne* of 3rd May 1811 announced a public auction of the complete collection on 4th June, including water-colours, drawings and prints by the painter himself, works he had been given in Italy by Gagneraux, Desprez and others, and works he had bought there. Among the latter were seven large paintings attributed to Annibale Carracci, Gherardo della Notte, Poussin, Bassano da Ponte, school of Domenichino and school of Rembrandt. Bids came in from Rome, Geneva, Zurich and Bern, and the lawyer Louis Porta proposed that the government should acquire part of the collection. A group of enlightened citizens led by Daniel-Alexandre Chavannes, also fearing the dispersal of this fine collection, suggested that a public subscription be opened to buy the complete collection and keep it until the government was in a position to acquire it. In so doing, the subscribers would 'thus facilitate the establishment of a school of drawing, an indispensable establishment in a town whose Academy brings together young people from diverse parts of the Canton'.

The bill of sale was signed on 11th July 1811 and the society of shareholders was made responsible for preserving the collection intact until its acquisition by the State of the Vaud. Among the shareholders was the canton itself, the towns of Lausanne and Vevey, the Academy, the Société d'Emulation and forty-three enthusiasts from all over Switzerland. In 1816 the subscribers had to remind the government of the pledge it had made, and the shareholders were finally reimbursed. An agreement was signed on 27th December 1816 and from that date Ducros' collection of paintings became the property of the State of the Vaud.

In this way, Ducros' works became the fine art section of the Musée Cantonal which already contained an important geological and zoological collection. In 1841 the studio collection was transferred and became the basis of the Musée des Beaux-Arts in Lausanne, which became the Musée Arlaud after the painter Marc-Louis Arlaud (1772–1845) donated a large sum for the construction of new premises (Bonjour, 1905). There were fifteen large Ducros water-colours on show there (manuscript catalogue, 1841), while the rest of the collection was bound and used for teaching. The school of drawing which Ducros had so strongly advocated at the beginning of the century could now be found in the Musée Arlaud, under the same roof as the Musée des Beaux-Arts.

This arrangement remained largely unchanged until 1906 (forty-five of Ducros' works on show in 1846, seventeen in 1876), when the collections went from the Musée Arlaud to the Palais de Rumine, where they remain today.

In 1953, thanks to the assiduity and discernment of the then curator, Monsieur Ernest Manganel, some of the large Ducros water-colours were taken out of store, cleaned and reframed. The quality of these works was recognized by the public at the exhibition in Lausanne in 1953, and in Rome in 1954. Thirty years later (1983–4) a new campaign was launched to clean the water-colours still in store (as discussed in the essay by Masson) and these works form the basis of the current exhibition.

But the rehabilitation of Ducros is far from being complete. Of the five hundred works by the painter in the possession of the Musée cantonal des Beaux-Arts, more than a hundred drawings, tracings, etchings and water-colours remain in uncatalogued portfolios. Lack of space and funds means that these works are kept in conditions far from conducive to their preservation. Must we wait for public subscription, as in 1811, in order to save them?

ANCIENT ROME

colour plate I

1

1 L'arc de Titus
The Arch of Titus

Pen and black ink, water-colour, heightened
with gouache, D & C BLAUW papers laid
down on canvas
$40\frac{1}{2} \times 26\frac{3}{8}$ in (103 × 67 cm)

Provenance : Studio collection, purchased by
public subscription in 1811, then by the State of
the Vaud in 1816. Musée Arlaud 1841; Musée
cantonal des Beaux-Arts, Lausanne, since 1906
Literature : Chessex, 1984 (2), fig p 74
Related works :—Pen and pencil drawing
(103 × 67 cm), Lausanne (MCBA)
—Water-colour, gouache and oil
(102 × 72·3 cm), Lausanne (MCBA)
—Pen and pencil drawing (100 × 65 cm),
Lausanne (MCBA), with note by William
Hamilton cit Chessex, 1984 (1), p 434
—Drawings and hand-coloured outline etchings
(c 74 × 50 cm), Stourhead, Wiltshire, the
Fondation Custodia, Paris and Christie's
2.11.1976 (490)

Lausanne, MCBA (Inv. D-816)

This triumphal arch at the top of the Via Sacra
is one of the sites most represented by artists,
particularly the side facing the Colosseum, as it
enabled them to include a view of the tower of
the Palazzo dei Conservatori on the Capitol in
the background. In his choice of viewpoint
Ducros was directly inspired by Panini's *Arch of
Titus* (1745, Museum of Fine Arts, Springfield
Mass., USA). Thirty years later the site itself
had changed little, but the way artists looked at
ruins had developed considerably. While Panini
limited the effects of time on the monument,
reconstructing the columns and inscriptions
without their cracks and splits, Ducros depicted
the ruined condition down to the smallest detail.
Playing with light and shade he painted every
crack, emphasizing the parts where pieces were
missing and covered it in spreading vegetation.
By choosing a vertical composition he
emphasised the monumental effect of the arch.
This is further reinforced by the very low
horizon and the way the sides seem to burst out
of the picture frame. Such realism is in contrast
to the impossible view of the Palazzo dei
Conservatori in the background which the artist
has placed towards the centre of the arch.
Apart from the two large views in Lausanne
only smaller versions sold to Sir Richard Colt
Hoare and Lord Ilchester, are known (see cat
no 73) but only technical examination can
determine whether these are hand-coloured
outline etchings or actual water-colours. An
engraving of this size is included in the list of
coloured prints from Ducros' studio (see
Appendix 2). According to Béat de Hennezel
(BCU) Ducros had a reputation for keeping his
large original paintings, selling only the hand-
coloured prints. Although this should not be
considered a hard and fast rule, the work under
consideration may support this theory. There is
a *terminus ante quem* for this view as Bridel in
the *Etrennes Helvétiennes* of 1790 says that he
admired a large *Arch of Titus* in Ducros' studio
in 1789. The style in which the figures are
painted, similar to those in the hand-coloured
outline etchings of 1780–84, would seem to
suggest an earlier date, between 1782 and 1785.
J H W Tischbein, J Vanderlyn and F Kaiserman
all painted very similar views clearly inspired by
Ducros.

2 L'arc de Constantin
The Arch of Constantine

Pen and black ink, water-colour, heightened
with gouache and oil, D & C BLAUW paper
laid down on canvas
$29\frac{1}{2} \times 42\frac{1}{4}$ in (74·8 × 107·5 cm)

Provenance : See no 1
Exhibited : Bern, 1810; Lausanne, 1953, no 2
Literature : Wagner, 1810, p 53; Agassiz, 1927,
p 37
Related works :—Full size version at Stourhead,
commissioned by Sir Richard Colt Hoare (see
cat no 71)
—Outline etching printed in reverse,
(50·3 × 72·3 cm), Lausanne (MCBA)

Lausanne, MCBA (Inv. D-817)

This is a replica of one of the last pictures Ducros painted for Sir Richard Colt Hoare (see cat no 71). The architectural details of the Colosseum and the Arch are identical in the Stourhead picture, but the surroundings are different: the dilapidated buildings on the right have been replaced by a wall; the left hand side has been completed with a view of the Temple of Venus and there are fewer figures. The *ancien-régime* style uniform of the soldiers suggests a date prior to Ducros' departure for Naples, but as the painter is known to have borrowed from earlier drawings costume is not a reliable means of dating his works. In any case, this water-colour cannot be dated any later than 1800, as Pius VII had the arch surrounded by a low wall in 1805, and Ducros did not return to Rome until 1806 (see cat no 6).

3   Vue du Colisée
View of the Colosseum

Pen and sepia ink, water-colour, heightened with gouache, papers laid down on canvas
31 × 46 in (78·7 × 116·7 cm)

Provenance: See no 1
Exhibited: Lausanne, 1953, no 3; Rome, 1954, no 2
Literature: Chessex, 1984 (1), fig 7
Related works:—Sketches, pen drawings squared for transfer, pencil drawings (same size), Lausanne (MCBA)
—Three pen and ink drawings of the same subject, reduced (54·5 × 75·5 cm), Lausanne (MCBA)
—Water-colour (43 × 64 cm), Earl of Ilchester, sold as Clérisseau, Sotheby's, 14.6.1973 (137)
—Water-colour, Sandon Hall, sold Sotheby's 21.2.1962 (189)

Lausanne, MCBA (Inv. D-823)

This monumental view of the northern side of the Colosseum is of documentary interest as it reveals one of the devices sometimes used by Ducros to reinforce perspective. The artist achieved a sense of grandeur through his choice of viewpoint, a 'wide angle' view of the ruin, and by carefully cutting out and gluing onto the sheet a separate painting of the left-hand side of the building. Foliage on the cut edges camouflages a technique which is not uncommon in Ducros' work and which he sometimes used to set elements of his landscapes literally into relief. To the same end he often covered the dark parts of the foreground with varnish. Besides masking joins, this also provided a contrast with the cool, matt tones of his background.

4   Intérieur du Colisée
Interior of the Colosseum

Pen and black ink, water-colour, heightened with gouache, D & C BLAUW paper laid down on canvas
29¾ × 44⅞ in (75·5 × 114 cm)

Provenance: See no 1
Literature: Agassiz, 1927, p 40 and 1928, fig 8; Chessex, 1984 (2) fig p 73
Related works:—Identical water-colour, commissioned by Sir Richard Colt Hoare, Stourhead, Wiltshire (see cat no 70)
—Pen and chalk drawing (79 × 117 cm),

colour plate II

colour plate III

Lausanne (MCBA)
—Several prints of an outline etching with their counter-proof, not coloured (53 × 74 cm), Lausanne (MCBA)
—A view of the Colosseum from a closer viewpoint and from the other side depicting the Via Crucis; hand-coloured outline etching from the Ducros and Volpato studio, 1780. The original drawing is signed and dated *Ducros fecit 1780*, Lausanne (MCBA)

Lausanne, MCBA (Inv. D-865)

The Colosseum has been put to many unlikely uses. For centuries it served as a quarry for building work, as a setting for various spectacles, as a barn, and as a saltpetre factory for the neighbouring gunpowder factory on the Palatine Hill. Under Pope Benedict XIV a monumental cross was erected at its centre and the Via Crucis constructed inside at the request of Leonardo da Porto Maurizio, a monk who had been preaching there since 1744. In 1756 the building was declared a public church and after 1783, when a new religious society was founded at the Colosseum, ceremonies filled the amphitheatre, as shown in this water-colour of circa 1787–88.
Colourful crowds were not the only aspect of the Colosseum to interest artists at this time. Philippe Secretan, a fellow Swiss visiting Rome, wrote in 1787: 'Here I am, I thought to myself, walking into the Colosseum where landscape painters should spend their days. This multitude of grottoes and porticoes, each lit in its own particular manner, this series of effects of light and shade becoming progressively more subdued, these mossy ruins covered in ivy, these hanging shrubs, the grand feelings inspired by this vast monument, . . . these all provide the finest object of study that a painter could hope to see'.[1]
Ducros often depicted the interior and exterior of the monument from different angles. A water-colour at Lausanne (MCBA), unusual in being signed and dated (1780), was the model for one of the set of *Vues de Rome et des ses environs* (1780). Some years later, around 1785–86, Ducros treated the same subject from another angle and with greater breadth in a water-colour bought by Sir Richard Colt Hoare of Stourhead (see cat no 70). The present work

is copied from the one at Stourhead in its architectural features, the figures having been left blank and redrawn later to allow for changes in women's dress. The two elegant ladies giving alms on the left of the picture bought by Colt Hoare are wearing the muslin dresses and straw hats of circa 1785–90, while in the unfinished work from Lausanne they appear more neo-classical with 'Directoire' hairstyles. During the same period L-J. Desprez, who worked with Ducros, made a sketch and water-colour of the same spot but from a higher viewpoint.[2] Ducros' very low viewpoint increases the monumentality of the amphitheatre, an effect further emphasized by the small figures. His liking for crowds can also be seen in several other works (see cat no 38). Despite the rather repetitive nature of the technique, the painter also succeeds in conveying the diversity of materials used in the construction of the Colosseum, including bricks, tuff, travertine and cobbles, as well as the variety of vegetation invading the ruins. But in no way does this attention to detail lessen the almost surreal character of a sunken ship that the amphitheatre seems to possess.

[1] P. Secretan, *Journal de voyage*, BCU, Fonds PELIS, Is. 4350.
[2] Wollin, 1935, figs 204 & 205.

5 Basilique de Maxence
The Basilica of Maxentius

Pen and sepia ink, water-colour, heightened with gouache, D & C BLAUW papers laid down on canvas
$31\frac{1}{2} \times 44\frac{1}{8}$ in (80 × 112 cm)

Provenance : See no 1
Literature : Agassiz, 1927, p 40; Chessex, 1984 (2), fig p 72
Related works :—Three pen drawings, slightly reduced (67 × 102 cm), Lausanne (MCBA)
—Pen drawing (52 × 73 cm), preparatory to the engraving, Lausanne (MCBA)
—Hand-coloured outline etching by Ducros and Volpato (52·5 × 73·2 cm)
—Water-colour, dated 1779 (52·9 × 73·8 cm), Yale Center for British Art, New Haven
—Water-colour (43·1 × 64·8 cm), The Whitworth Art Gallery, Manchester (see cat no 64)

Lausanne, MCBA (Inv. D-846)

In the eighteenth century these huge vaults in the Forum were known as the Temple of Peace, and the engraving of the site by Ducros and Volpato from 1780 is labelled *Temple de la Paix*. In a report on the state of the Forum made for Napoleon in 1809 this name is still given to the Basilica of Maxentius, which was completed by Constantine.
The composition of this landscape, with part of Santa Maria Nova (Santa Francesca Romana) on the extreme right, seems to have been created by a camera obscura and a wide-angle lens. We know that Ducros used such devices for his architectural drawings,[1] but he often altered the proportions of the buildings when at work on the composition in his studio. In composition the Ducros/Volpato engraving and this large water-colour are identical but the same cannot be said of the comparable drawings in Manchester and New Haven. The more expansive treatment of this water-colour together with the style of the unfinished figures

suggests that the drawing dates from 1784–86 and was taken up again at a later date.

[1] 'He made continual use of the camera obscura and had several of them, and he needed quite a retinue to carry his apparatus' (letter from De la Rive to his wife, 24.5.1812, cit Baud-Bovy, 1903 p 163).

6 Vue générale du Palatin avec l'arc de Constantin
General view of the Palatine Hill with the Arch of Constantine

Water-colour heightened with gouache, pen and black ink for the figures, D & C BLAUW papers laid down on canvas
$30\frac{1}{8} \times 49\frac{7}{8}$ in (76·6 × 126·6 cm)

Provenance: See no 1
Literature: Agassiz, 1927, p 40

Lausanne, MCBA (Inv. D-851)

6

This panoramic view sweeps from Santi Giovanni e Paolo on the extreme left to the Arch of Constantine in the centre with the remains of the Aqua Claudia in the background, to the Palatine Hill covered in rich vegetation on the right. The Temple of Venus on the right, with its characteristic vaulting is only present through artistic licence, as it in fact stands out of view to the right.
This is one of the last works Ducros produced in Italy during his visit in 1806 before he finally returned to Switzerland. This is confirmed by the small wall surrounding the triumphal arch, which cannot be found in any of the earlier pictures of this site (see, for example, cat no 2). The Arch had been cleared up and surrounded with a protective wall by Pius VII in 1805, and the barrier was only destroyed in 1829.[1]
The picture has qualities typical of Ducros: the precision of detail (the vegetation in the foreground, the little hut on the right), the added figures (here left unpainted), the delicacy of the cool shades of the background (particularly the Aqua Claudia), and a notable liking for vegetation spread over every element of the landscape, shown in a rather repetitive and laboured manner.

[1] E. Rodocanachi, *Les monuments de Rome*, Paris, 1914, p 141.

the Palatine Hill in the background. To the left of the arch are the buildings destroyed during archaeological excavations in the Forum in the last century.
This is the original drawing from which Ducros and Volpato made the etching of *L'arc de Septime-Sévère,* one of the set of views of Rome (1780). The print contains slightly fewer figures, and has a different background showing the columns of the Temple of Saturn.
As is often the case with these views of Rome made for travellers on the Grand Tour, the picture works on two levels: as a topographical view of a famous monument and as a picturesque illustration of Roman life, with beggars, pilgrims, peasants and fashionable ladies. It is worth noting that Ducros' compatriot Jacques Sablet had acquired something of a reputation in Rome for his genre scenes, and that the two were to collaborate in 1782–83 on the publication of a set of aquatint scenes from Italian daily life.[1]

[1] Nantes, Lausanne, Rome, exhibition catalogue, 1985, pp 100–108.

7 L'arc de Septime-Sévère
The Arch of Septimius Severus

Pen and black ink, grey wash and water-colour, J HONIG & ZOONEN paper
$20\frac{5}{8} \times 29\frac{1}{8}$ in (52·5 × 74 cm)

Inscribed (on the figure on the right): *brun obsc*
Provenance: See no 1
Exhibited: Lausanne, 1953, no 8; Rome, 1954, no 7
Literature: Agassiz, 1927, p 36; Chessex, 1984 (1), fig 2
Related works:—Hand-coloured outline etching by Volpato and Ducros (52 × 74 cm)

Lausanne, MCBA (Inv. D-873)

This view was taken from the terrace of San Giuseppe dei Falegnami, the church on the right, which overlooks the Campo Vaccino. The Arch of Septimius Serverus can be seen on the left, while the House of Augustus is visible on

7

8

8 Vue générale du Campo Vaccino
General view of the Campo Vaccino

Pen and black ink, grey wash and water-colour,
J HONIG & ZOONEN paper
21 × 29 in (53·1 × 73·7 cm)

Provenance: See no 1
Exhibited: Lausanne, 1953, no 19, Rome, 1954,
no 18
Literature: Agassiz, 1927, p 36 and 1928, fig 10
Related works:—Drawing (54 × 75 cm),
Lausanne (MCBA)
—Hand-coloured outline etching by Ducros
and Volpato (50 × 73 cm)

Lausanne, MCBA (Inv. D-888)

This view down onto the Roman Forum from
the base of the Capitoline Hill has long been
popular with artists and occurs in Piranesi's
Vedute. This is one of Ducros' very rare
drawings from nature, and includes none of the
figures that were usually added later at his
studio.
The Arch of Septimius Severus is shown half-
buried, and there is a good view of the Campo
Vaccino (Field of Cows), so called until the

nineteenth century as it served as a cattle
market.
The left side is defined by a row of houses
wedged between the churches of Santi Martina
e Luca and San Lorenzo in Miranda (Temple of
Antoninus and Faustina). At the far end of the
Campo is a convent, extending from Santa
Maria Nova at the Arch of Titus (the entrance)
to, on the right, the walls of the Farnese
Gardens on the Palatine and the houses grouped
around Santa Maria Liberatrice at the foot of
the House of Augustus. The Fountain of
Giuturna, Column of Phocas and the three
columns of the Temple of Castor and Pollux at
the centre were the only other ancient ruins
visible at the time. In the Napoleonic era this
space again became known as the Forum and
the last century saw the full archaeological
excavation of the ruins.
Both a drawing of the same site and the hand-
coloured outline etching by Ducros and Volpato
include the columns of the Temple of Saturn in
the right foreground, which obstruct the view of
the Palatine. This composition was also adopted
by Ducros for the painting at Pavlovsk showing
Grand Duke Paul in the Forum (1782, fig P, see
cat no 56).

9 Vue de l'intérieur du Capitole
View within the Capitol

Outline etching, pen and black ink, water-
colour, C & I HONIG paper
$20\frac{7}{16} × 29\frac{1}{4}$ in (51·8 × 74·5 cm) sheet size
$20\frac{1}{8} × 29\frac{1}{8}$ in (51·2 × 74 cm) image size

Inscribed (b.l.): *L. Antino/li; n. Righi*
Provenance: See no 1
Exhibited: Lausanne, 1953, no 12; Rome, 1954,
no 11
Related works:—Water-colour, pen and ink
(52·8 × 73·7 cm), Lausanne (MCBA), model for
the print (fig. A)
—*Vue du Capitole,* hand-coloured outline
etching with letters (b.r., inside the border),
Lausanne (MCBA), Weimar Goethemuseum,
Hermitage, Drottningholm, British Museum
and Private Collection (fig B)

Lausanne, MCBA (Inv. D-879)

The Piazza del Campidoglio has often been
depicted by artists, but seldom from this angle.
Here the Dioscuri and the Trophies of Marius
are seen from behind, set against the sky; the
brick facade of Santa Maria d'Aracoeli is also
visible.
This etching, a first impression before letters,
belongs to the set of *Vues de Rome et des ses
environs* published by Ducros and Volpato in
1780. As a working proof, it has been only
partly painted in water-colour and this allows us
to study Ducros' technique in action. The
original drawing from Lausanne (fig A) is
identical as far as the architecture is concerned,
but it lacks some of the figures, namely the men
at work on the left and right and the women
passing by. It corresponds with the first printed
version, but is not coloured. To this first proof
Ducros has added several figures decorating the
piazza. The figures of Antinoli and Righi on the
scaffolding can be identified from the 'n' and 'L'
above their respective heads, which seems to
suggest that the scene was taken from life. On
the final print (fig B; both coloured and plain
examples are known), the engraver kept some

9

fig. A
Ducros,
Vue du Capitole (water-
colour), Lausanne
(MCBA).

fig. B
Volpato and Ducros,
Vue du Capitole (hand-
coloured outline
etching). Private
Collection, Zurich.

figures but omitted others (namely the men on
the scaffolding and those holding the winch).
This work highlights the ambiguous status of
the gouache, oil, and hand-coloured outline
etchings that Ducros produced.[1] Different states
are not readily distinguishable, particularly
when features were added by hand, as is
sometimes the case with prints from the Ducros/
Volpato studio.

10 Intérieur des Thermes de Caracalla
Interior of the Baths of Caracalla

Grey wash and water-colour over pencil,
J HONIG & ZOONEN paper
$20\frac{3}{4} \times 29\frac{1}{4}$ in (52·8 × 74·5 cm)

Provenance: See no 1
Exhibited: Lausanne, 1953, no 18; Rome, 1954,
no 17
Literature: Agassiz, 1927, p 36

Lausanne, MCBA (Inv. D-885)

[1] See Van de Sandt, 1980, on this subject.

10

This view was drawn in the middle room (the *Tepidarium*) of the Baths of Caracalla. The arches of the ruin are depicted with great precision. The foundations of the building were only exposed in the nineteeth century, hence the ground level depicted is very high and the site is covered in vegetation. The sole liberty taken by the painter is the view towards the Aventine Hill through the arched doorway, as the Baths had a surrounding wall. Ducros seems to have had a special liking for this site; he made two hand-coloured etchings of it (see cat no 67) and there are several drawings of the Baths from various angles, particularly two very fine water-colours at the Museé de Berne. This interest may be partly explained by the fact that in 1779 his colleague Volpato obtained permission from Pius VI to carry out excavations on the site. This view must date from Ducros' early days in Rome (1778–1780) as there is a lack of boldness in the foliage (the branches still being underlined with a black brush-stroke), while the figures are merely imprecise silhouettes.

MODERN ROME

Ducros rarely painted modern Rome, the exceptions being the Trevi Fountain, the entrance to the Farnese Gardens on the Palatine

and the Temple of Aesculapius built in the Borghese Gardens by Asprucci in 1786. However, he did paint a set of seven views of Roman villas or their gardens (cat nos 11–17), which he etched and published with Volpato around 1782–84. Nearly all the drawings for these are in the Lausanne studio collection. In the last century they were subjected to a great deal of use and exhibited with no protection and have thus lost some of their original colour. But they are still of interest as examples of Ducros' first style: a synthesis of topographical view and genre scene. They also reveal how the artist divided his work even then, as the architecture was clearly drawn first, and the figures added later (see in particular cat nos 11 and 12).

11   Les jardins de Palazzo Doria Pamphili
The gardens of the Palazzo Doria Pamphili

Pen and black ink, grey wash, water-colour heightened with gouache, J HONIG & ZOONEN paper
21 × 29¼ in (53·2 × 74·4 cm)

Provenance: See no 1
Exhibited: Lausanne, 1953 no 7; Rome, 1954, no 6
Literature: Huber, 1800, IV, p 218; Agassiz, 1927, p 35 and fig 8; Agassiz, 1928, fig 4
Related works: —Hand-coloured outline etching by Volpato and Ducros

Lausanne MCBA (Inv. D-872)

For the print Ducros abandoned the maudlin episode of the drowned woman, retaining only the elegant figures and the exotic group. There is a remarkable similarity between the viewpoint of Ducros' drawing and that of a large painting of the same location painted by Vernet for the Marquis de Villette in 1746[1] and sold to Catherine the Great who gave it to the Acadamy of St. Petersburg in 1768. Ducros may have known it from an engraving.

[1]   Ingersoll-Smouse, *Joseph Vernet*, Paris, 1926, fig 51.

12   Villa Montalto-Negroni

Pen and black ink, grey wash and water-colour, J HONIG & ZOONEN paper
20¾ × 29 in (52·8 × 73·7 cm)
(verso: sketch of an unidentified villa, pencil)

Provenance: See no 1
Exhibited: Lausanne, 1953, no 10 (as the Villa Borghese); Rome, 1954, no 9
Literature: Huber, 1800, IV, p 218; Agassiz, p 35 (as the Villa Borghese); Chessex, 1984(1), fig 3
Related works: —Hand-coloured outline etching by Volpato and Ducros (cat no 66)

Lausanne, MCBA (Inv. D-877)

The figures were retained in the etching which includes an additional group of three figures entering the villa. This has since been demolished.

13   Les jardins de Palazzo Corsini
The gardens of the Palazzo Corsini

Grey wash, water-colour, heightened with

11

gouache over outline etching, J HONIG &
ZOONEN paper
$20\frac{3}{4} \times 29\frac{1}{4}$ in ($52 \cdot 9 \times 74 \cdot 3$ cm) sheet size
$20\frac{3}{8} \times 29\frac{1}{4}$ in ($51 \cdot 8 \times 74 \cdot 2$ cm) image size

Provenance: Purchased in 1928

Lausanne, MCBA (Inv. D-880)

The original drawing on which this print is
based is unlocated. The Palazzo Corsini can be
seen below the gardens, while the dome of Sant
Andrea della Valle and the characteristic outline
of the Pantheon may be distinguished in the
background. This view may still be seen today
by going up to the Botanical Gardens just below
the Janiculum. Rarely are the scenes of Rome so
well preserved!

14 Palazzina Borghese

Pen and black ink, grey wash and water-colour,
J HONIG & ZOONEN paper
21×29 in ($53 \cdot 2 \times 73 \cdot 8$ cm)

Provenance: See no 1
Exhibited: Lausanne, 1953 no 14; Rome, 1954,
no 13
Literature: Agassiz, 1927, p 35 and 1928, fig 5;
Chessex, 1982, p 56 and fig 3 (mistakenly
described as a hand-coloured outline etching)
Related works: —Hand-coloured outline
etching by Volpato and Ducros

Lausanne, MCBA (Inv. D-881)

The only real differences between the drawing
and etching lie in details, such as the costumes
of the young women on the right. The group of
dancing girls bears a resemblance to the
bacchantes in ancient paintings from
Herculaneum, which inspired several of Ducros'
friends around 1780 including Flaxman and
Canova.[1]

[1] D. Irwin, 1979, pp 48–51. For the relationship between
Flaxman and Ducros see cat no 75.

15 Les jardins de Villa Médicis
The gardens of the Villa Medici

Pen and black ink, grey wash and water-colour,
C & I HONIG paper
$20\frac{7}{8} \times 29$ in ($53 \times 73 \cdot 5$ cm)

Provenance: See no 1
Exhibited: Lausanne, 1953, no 16 (as a Roman
villa); Rome, 1954, no 15
Literature: Huber, 1800, IV, p 218; Agassiz,
1927, pp 12, 35 and 1928, fig 1
Related works: —Hand-coloured outline
etching by Ducros and Volpato

Lausanne, MCBA (Inv. D-884)

The pines in the gardens of the Villa Borghese
can be seen behind the obelisk. There are no
notable differences between the drawing and the
etching.

16 Les jardins de Villa Colonna
The gardens of the Villa Colonna

Pen and black ink, grey wash and water-colour,
J HONIG & ZOONEN paper
$20\frac{1}{2} \times 29$ in ($52 \times 73 \cdot 8$ cm)

12

13

14

15

16

17

Provenance: See no 1
Exhibited: Lausanne, 1953, no 17 (as the gardens of a Roman villa); Rome, 1954, no 16
Literature: Huber, 1800, IV p 218; Agassiz, 1927, p 35 (as the gardens of the Villa Medici) and 1928, fig 3
Related works: —Hand-coloured outline etching by Ducros and Volpato

Lausanne, MCBA (Inv. D-886)

Facing south, we see the bottom of the Colonna Gardens with picturesque groups of figures and the Torre delle Milizie in the background.

17   Villa Ludovisi

Pen and black ink, grey wash and water-colour, J HONIG & ZOONEN paper
$14\frac{1}{2} \times 21$ in (36.9×53.2 cm)

Provenance: See no 1
Exhibited: Lausanne, 1953, no 22 (as the Villa Medici); Rome, 1954, no 21
Literature: Agassiz, 1928, fig 2
Related works: —Hand-coloured outline etching by Ducros and Volpato

Lausanne, MCBA (Inv. D-892)

The facade of the Villa Ludovisi (now demolished) is here viewed from an angle that reveals the Palazzo Barberini in the background. There are only minute differences in the engraving which is smaller in format than others in the series and may have been published separately.

CENTRAL ITALY

18   Vue de Tivoli avec le Temple de la Sibylle
View of Tivoli with the Temple of the Sibyl

Water-colour, heightened with gouache and oil, D & C BLAUW papers laid down on canvas
$26\frac{1}{4} \times 40\frac{1}{8}$ in (66.7×102 cm)

Inscribed: (in brush on the reverse of the original canvas): *Tyvoli = /Tempio della Sybilla = della parte del fiume/Vicino a Roma*
Provenance: See no 1
Exhibited: Lausanne, 1953, no 25
Literature: Chessex, 1984 (1), fig 9
Related works: —ink drawing squared for transfer (54×75 cm), an exact reduction of the large view and probably a preparatory sketch for the etching, Lausanne (MCBA)
—See following entry for another version.

Lausanne, MCBA (Inv. D-798)

Like the majority of artists living in Rome, Ducros went to Tivoli each summer to escape the heat. In a letter to Charles Bonnet (1783) he explains how he was more at ease when alone at Tivoli and directly in touch with nature than he was in the company of the Pope's courtiers. The reputation Ducros enjoyed around 1785 is clear from articles in local journals and travellers' memoirs, and was based primarily on his depictions of waterfalls, particularly those at Tivoli. 'In the falls of the Anio, he has tried to express the movement the wind gives to the

water as it falls and to the vapours which rise
from it, and he has done so with great success'
(*Memorie*, 1785). Such was the success of his
views of waterfalls that they can now be found
in many collections (Stourhead, Dunham
Massey, Stratfield Saye and various private
collections). The studio collection in Lausanne,
however, contains only preparatory sketches for
these subjects.

This painting shows the Temple of the Sibyl and
the Anio upstream from the famous falls. The
spray can be seen beneath the bridge. This
viewpoint is rare and was previously used in an
etching from the early 1780s (see cat no 20).
A later version of this large water-colour (see cat
no 19) shows how the painter could give the
same landscape a totally different character.
When a compatriot of his admired a painting of
the Temple of the Sibyl in his studio in 1787 and
complimented him on the treatment of the sky,
Ducros remarked: 'The sky . . . is to a landscape
what the face is to a human figure; it is the sky
which, by accidents of light and shade, spreads
over the landscape tones of sadness or gaiety,
sombreness or serenity, peace or agitation, as
befits the character one wants to depict'.[1] In
keeping with this, the serene small landscape
with its washerwomen wearing the traditional
headwear of *amandille* (see cat no 19) becomes
more disturbing in this larger water-colour
where stormy weather creates contrasts of light
and shade. The women in peasant costume have
gone, and in their place is a scene which was
something of a *leitmotif* in certain landscapes
from the 1790s: a hidden man blending with the
vegetation (on the left) watching women doing
their washing (compare cat no 21).

[1]   Philippe Secretan. *Journal de voyage*, BCU, Fonds
PELIS, Is 4350, fol 61.

18

19   Vue de Tivoli avec le Temple de la Sibylle
View of Tivoli with the Temple of the Sibyl

Pen and sepia ink, water-colour
D & C BLAUW paper
21 × 29¼ in (53·2 × 74·2 cm)

Provenance: See no 1
Related works: —Pencil drawing strengthened
with charcoal, in reverse (54·5 × 75·5 cm),
squared for transfer onto copperplate,
Lausanne (MCBA)
—See previous entry

Lausanne, MCBA (Inv. D-906)

19

20   Temple de la Sibylle à Tivoli
Temple of the Sibyl, Tivoli

Hand-coloured outline etching,
J HONIG & ZOONEN paper
20⅝ × 29 in (52·3 × 73·8 cm) sheet size
20¼ × 28⅝ in (51·6 × 72·8 cm) image size

Provenance: See no 1
Exhibited: Lausanne, 1953, no 27; Rome, 1954,
no 26
Literature: Agassiz, 1927, p 38

Lausanne, MCBA (Inv. D-887)

In all the etchings from the *Vues de Rome et de
ses environs* series by Ducros and Volpato
differences occur due to the colouring by hand.

20

21

Some prints have stronger contrasts, others have figures added where there are no etched lines, as is the case with this etching of Tivoli. Another print, at the Hermitage in Leningrad[1] includes the Virgin and Child on the parapet of the bridge, which cannot be seen in this work.

[1] The Print Room of the Hermitage has a complete set of views by Ducros and Volpato, with some duplicates. Our thanks to Mr Y. Roussakov, Chief Curator of the Gallery, for this reference.

21   Intérieur de la Villa de Mécène à Tivoli
Interior of the Villa of Maecenas, Tivoli

Pen and black ink, remains of varnish,
D & C BLAUW paper
$21\frac{3}{16} \times 29\frac{1}{4}$ in (53·8 × 74·4 cm)

Provenance: See no 1
Literature: Chessex, 1984 (2), fig p 75
Related works: —Pen drawing on tracing paper (55 × 76 cm), Lausanne
—Water-colour (74·9 × 107·9 cm), Stourhead (see cat no 69)
—Pen drawing on tracing paper (77 × 113 cm), Lausanne (MCBA)

Lausanne, MCBA (Inv. D-907)

The ruins of the Santuario di Ercole Vincitore or Temple of Hercules (1st century B.C.) had long been considered to be the remains of the Villa of Maecenas, a monumental complex at Tivoli beside the ancient Via Tiburtina. Shortly after 1786, Ducros painted a large water-colour of the Villa of Maecenas for Sir Richard Colt Hoare, who described it as a 'souterrain view' (see cat no 69). As usual, Ducros kept a large tracing and produced a reduced version from which he probably intended to make a coloured etching. This site features in the list of views Ducros sold on the Strada della Croce (see Appendix 2), but no print of it is known. The women discovered bathing both by the viewer and by the three men on the extreme right, provides a secular version of the story of Susanna (see cat no 18).

22

22   Temple d'Hercule à Tivoli
Temple of Hercules, Tivoli

Water-colour, the figures heightened in gouache, J WHATMAN papers laid down on canvas
$30\frac{1}{4} \times 43\frac{7}{8}$ in (76·5 × 111·5 cm)

Inscribed (in brush on the reverse of the original canvas): *Le Temple d'Hercule Tyvoly*
Provenance: See no 1
Exhibited: Lausanne, 1953, no 28
Literature: Agassiz, 1927, p 40; Chessex, 1982

Lausanne, MCBA (Inv. D-838)

This is another view of the ruins of the Temple of Hercules, or Villa of Maecenas (see previous entry). In his *Darstellungen aus Italien*, 1792,[1] Meyer described the beauties of Tivoli's landscape as *pittoresques*, and defined what he meant as tranquil grandeur: mountains covered with ruins and undergrowth, and fine views of the valley. All these elements can be seen in this water-colour by Ducros with the size and composition adding a sense of sublime grandeur. The view through an arch or the arch of a bridge was a compositional device he

23

I. *L'arc de Titus* cat 1

II. (above):   *L'arc de Constantin* cat 2

III. (below):   *Vue du Colisée* cat 3

IV. (above):   *Temple de Jupiter Sérapis à Pouzzoles* cat 31

V. (below):   *Intérieur de l'Amphithéâtre à Pouzzoles* cat 32

VI. *Cascata delle Marmore* (Terni) cat 25

VII. *Eruption du Vésuve et naufrage* cat 37

VIII. (above):   *Vue des Temples de Paestum* cat 40

IX. (below):   *Tombeau de Virgile (Pausilippe)* cat 35

X. (above): *Vue du Grand Port de la Valette* cat 45

XI. (below): *Fontaine de Neptune et Marché aux Poissons à la Valette* cat 44

XII. *Orage nocturne à Cefalù* cat 41

favoured and can be found in several of his
paintings (see cat nos 49 & 50), and in the work
of Hubert Robert.

[1]   Elisabeth Chevalier, *Les tableaux d'Italie de Friedrich
Johann Lorenz Meyer*, Naples, 1980, p 136.

23   Vue du Ponte Lucano et du tombeau de la famille Plautia
View of the Ponte Lucano and of the Plautian
Family Tomb

Water-colour heightened with gouache, remains
of varnish, D & C BLAUW paper laid down on
canvas
$25\frac{5}{8} \times 39\frac{3}{8}$ in (65 × 100 cm)

Provenance: See no 1
Literature: Agassiz, 1927, p 37
Related works: —Water-colour (65 × 100·5 cm),
Stourhead, almost identical.
—*Vue du Ponte Lucano*, 1806, commissioned by
F von Sachsen-Gotha (unlocated)
—Pen and pencil drawing (54·5 × 75·5 cm),
Lausanne (MCBA)
—Pen drawing with border (36·4 × 52·4 cm),
preparatory sketch for an etching, Lausanne
(MCBA)

Lausanne, MCBA (Inv. D-818)

Coming from Rome towards Tivoli, just before
the road rises through olive trees, the Ponte
Lucano crosses the River Anio and leads to the
tomb constructed by the consul Plautius
Silvanus. It is cylindrical in form, like the tomb
of Cecilia Metella, and faced with blocks of
travertine (the *lapis tiburtinus* of classical times)
taken from the quarries of the region used for
the Colosseum and St. Peter's. The tomb has
been altered over the centuries, the upper
ramparts being a medieval addition.
A similar view bought by Sir Richard Colt
Hoare of Stourhead in 1786 may be a copy or
the original version. The outlines of the
buildings and the general composition are the
same in each, with differences in the
backgrounds and in the distribution of light and
shade. The more dramatic contrasts in tone in
the sky and mountains of the Lausanne version

24

suggest a later date than the Stourhead picture.
Ducros also painted a *Ponte Lucano* in 1806 for
Friedrich von Sachsen-Gotha. Guattani tells us
that the picture 'presents a fine spring morning,
near the Ponte Lucano; in the middle distance
stands the mausoleum of the Plautia family, and
further away are the Apennines and the ruins of
the Villa Adriana'.[1] The site of the Villa
Adriana cannot be seen in the Stourhead and
Lausanne pictures.

[1]   Guattani, *Memorie*, II, 1807, p 72.

24   Vue idéale avec Rocca Pia
Imaginary view with the Rocca Pia

Pen and black ink, water-colour, heightened
with gouache, remains of varnish,
J WHATMAN papers laid down on canvas
$31\frac{1}{2} \times 49\frac{1}{4}$ in (80 × 125 cm)

Inscribed (with a brush on the back of the
original canvas): *Vue du Tibre. S Bartolo. Pont
Rompu. Pour Monsieur Irving no 8 Harley
Foreman*
Provenance: See no 1
Literature: Agassiz, 1927, p 37
Related works: —*The Ponte Rotto, Rome*
(82·5 × 124·5 cm), Victoria & Albert Museum
(fig C)
—*Ponte Rotto*, Galleria S Giorgi, Rome, 1913

fig. C
Ducros,
*The Ponte Rotto,
Rome*, Victoria and
Albert Museum,
London.

Lausanne, MCBA (Inv. D-828)

This imaginary landscape contains a very precise representation of the Rocca Pia, a fifteenth-century fortress still standing in Tivoli. The Roman artist Carlo Labruzzi (who also worked for Colt Hoare) made a drawing of the same site[1] and in the 1850s Robert Macpherson took a photograph from the same spot.[2] Both the photograph and the drawing show that Ducros' portrayal is precise but for the moat of the castle (which has become two branches of a river, making the Rocca into an island) while on the left he has added part of a ruined arch. The island and the broken arch recall another site, the Isola Tibertina and the Ponte Rotto. Ducros had painted a view of the Tiber at Rome with the famous Ponte Rotto and the Isola Tibertina, but this painting is known only through a photograph (Galleria San Giorgi, Rome, 1913). The inscription, which was on the reverse of the original canvas, becomes less mysterious if one identifies 'Monsieur Irving' with James Irvine, an historical painter and picture dealer known to most English artists in Rome circa 1781–91.[3] He may be the same as the 'Sigr. Joring' whose name is on the back of a painting by Ducros at the Victoria & Albert Museum (fig C). The various elements of the painting in London can be seen to result from the superimposition of these two earlier pictures as it shows the Ponte Rotto with the Isola Tiberina, crowned with the Rocco Pia, and, rather unexpectedly in this Roman context, the Sabine Hills.

[1]   *Roma, Paessaggi, vedute e costumi*, Gasparrini-Chaucer, Rome-London, 1983, fig 72c.
[2]   *Paessaggio, Immagine e Realtà*, Galleria Communale d'Arte Moderna, Bologna, 1981–82, fig 355.
[3]   C F Bell, *Annals of Thomas Banks*, Cambridge, 1938, pp 28, 165.

25 Cascata delle Marmore (Terni)
The Marble Cascade, Terni

Pen and black ink, water-colour, heightened with gouache and oil, D & C BLAUW papers laid on canvas
38⅛ × 29 in (96·8 × 73·7 cm)

colour plate VI

58   25

Provenance: See no 1
Literature: Chessex, 1982, p 57 and 1984 (1), p 432
Related works: —Pen and pencil drawing, squared for transfer (101 × 67 cm), inscribed: *cascata di Terni in primo piano*, Lausanne (MCBA)
Several versions of the 'Cascata di Terni in secondo piano' (Lausanne, Stourhead, Dunham Massey); see cat no 72

Lausanne, MCBA (Inv. D-814)

The falls of the Velino in the Nera near Terni in Umbria, better known as the *Cascata delle Marmore* was one of the essential sights for travellers visiting Italy, and is often described in enthusiastic terms.[1] Lalande, for example, wrote: 'I think that apart from the Niagara falls in America there is no such beautiful waterfall'.[2] But it was not a popular subject with artists until the last quarter of the eighteenth century, and J P Hackert and Ducros were among the first to paint large pictures of the cascade. In 1785 Lord Grey noted in his journal 'We went to see the paintings of Mr du Cros a landscape painter who seems to have a good deal of merit. His views of the Fall of Terni are much admired. . . .'[3] Around 1785, Ducros was celebrated in Rome for his depictions of the waterfalls at Terni and Tivoli. As early as 1783 the painter remarked in a letter to his Genevan patron, the naturalist Charles Bonnet: 'Ah! How I prefer to be beneath the cascades of Tivoli at sunrise where Newton could split light without a prism. . . .'[4] The *Memorie per le Belle Arti* (1785) reports thus:'. . . He has just painted for Lord Breadalbane the two famous waterfalls of the Velino and the Anio, and, by choosing a judicious viewpoint for both avoids the sense of terror that such subjects usually inspire. . . .'
Sir Richard Colt Hoare was also impressed by the artist's gift for painting waterfalls, and of *The Falls of the Velino into the River Nera* (cat no 72) remarked: 'One of the great excellences of the artist was the just and natural delineation of water, particularly where spray and vapour were expressed; and in this subject he has succeeded most admirably, and without any of the borrowed assistance of white paint'.[5]
In this version, seen from a closer position than the one at Stourhead, the waterfall takes on even greater importance in the structure of the picture. Without sacrificing details (for instance the small observation point, above right, constructed by Pius VI in 1781), Ducros organized his composition to obtain the maximum monumental effect: little is seen of the sky and the tiny figures are relegated to the bottom of the picture. In this composition Ducros translated into a single image Meyer's description of 1792: 'There exist in the ancient world cataracts much more considerable in size, . . . but none unites the different characteristics of height, abundance, picturesque surroundings, to the same degree as this Niagara of Italy'.[6]

[1]   Ludwig Schudt, *Italienreisen im 17. und 18. Jahrhundert*, Vienna and Munich, 1959, pp 178–179.
[2]   Jérôme de Lalande, *Voyage en Italie*, Paris, 1786, vol 8, p 47.
[3]   *A Journal of my Tour on the Continent in the years 1784 and 1785*, 16th March, 1785, fol 81–82; diary owned by Lord Wilton, on loan to Manchester City Art Gallery, reference kindly provided by Michael Clarke.
[4]   Letter from Ducros to Bonnet, 7th July 1783, BPU.
[5]   *History of Modern Wiltshire*, 1822, p 83.
[6]   Elisabeth Chevalier, op cit, p 53.

26 Vue de Capistrello (Abruzzes)
View of Capistrello, the Abruzzi

Water-colour, the figures heightened in
gouache, D & C BLAUW paper laid down on
canvas
$26\frac{3}{8} \times 41$ in $(67 \times 104$ cm)

Inscribed (in brush on the reverse of the original
canvas): *Vüe de Capestrelle/Province d'abruzzo
Royau. Naples*
Provenance: See no 1
Exhibited: Lausanne, 1953, no 34; Rome, 1954,
no 29
Literature: Agassiz, 1927, p 42

Lausanne, MCBA (Inv. D-806)

When Ducros was banished from Rome in
February 1793, he took refuge for several
months on the outer edges of the Papal States,
in the Abruzzi, part of the Kingdom of Naples.
Six water-colours preserved in Lausanne
(MCBA) were painted in the Roveto Valley
where the River Liri flows, and Ducros
probably painted them at this time. They were
completed in Naples by the mysterious assistant
whose elegant figures can be found in the
majority of the large water-colours from
Ducros' Neapolitan period.
The site depicted here has neither the
atmosphere nor the iconographic tradition of
Tivoli, and tourists did not visit the Abruzzi in
such large numbers as they did the Anio, Velino
or Nera rivers. Perhaps this explains why, unlike
the majority of the large water-colours
commissioned by English patrons, tracings and
squared drawings of these views of the Abruzzi
do not exist in Ducros' studio collection. Unable
to sell them, Ducros brought these water-
colours back to Lausanne towards the end of his
life.
The site depicted here is the village of
Capistrello with the Liri at its foot. This wild
landscape can still be seen today, although
much altered by new buildings and roads. The
turbulent water and rocks covered in vegetation
echo themes the painter made his own during
the peak of his career in Rome. Ducros treated
the Liri as if it were the Anio and the wild rocks
of the Abruzzi as if they were stones from the
monuments of Ancient Rome.

26

27

27 Source dans les Abruzzes
A spring in the Abruzzi

Water-colour, the figures heightened in
gouache, D & C BLAUW paper laid down on
canvas
$26\frac{3}{4} \times 41$ in $(68 \times 104$ cm)

Inscribed (in brush on the reverse of the original
canvas): *Les sources du Velino/a Taglia C.
abruzzo*
Provenance: See no 1
Exhibited: Lausanne, 1953, no 36
Literature: Agassiz, 1927, p 41; Chessex, 1984
(2), fig p 71

Lausanne, MCBA (Inv. D-836)

The paths cut by rivers and streams around
Tagliacozze in the Abruzzi are typical of
limestone terrain, producing numerous grottoes
and springs, including the Imele, Velino and Liri
rivers. There may have been some confusion
over the names when Ducros was in the region

28

or when he wrote the title on the back of the canvas, as this is not in fact the source of the Velino, but a reappearance of the Imele very near Tagliacozze (see *Attraverso l'Italia. Abruzzo e Molise*, Milan, 1948, p 71, fig 107; also Mario Fondi, *Le regioni d'Italia*, vol 12, Turin, 1970, p 124).

Comparison between the painting and photographs makes the precision of Ducros' depiction of the rocks strikingly clear. The true subject of this water-colour is not the spring itself but the rough rock-face. Ducros has painted it with great finesse in all the variety of its greys, greens, ochres and yellows.

28   Arbres dans les Abruzzes
Trees in the Abruzzi

Water-colour, the figures in pen and black ink, D & C BLAUW paper laid down on canvas
$26\frac{3}{4} \times 40\frac{1}{2}$ in (67 × 103 cm)

Provenance: See no 1
Exhibited: Lausanne, 1953, no 37; Rome, 1954, no 30; Naples, 1962 (ex-catalogue)
Literature: Agassiz, 1927, p 42

Lausanne, MCBA (Inv. D-837)

This study of trees was made near the small village of Corcumello. A few of its houses can be seen on the right and Mount Velino rises in the background (site identified by Signor Renzo Mancini, Soprintendente per i beni ambientali per l'Abruzzo, Aquila). Although the identification of the site may seem purely incidental, it does suggest that this water-colour was actually painted from nature and thus provides some indication of Ducros' position in the history of landscape painting. Artists at the time often painted in the open air, a practice encouraged from about 1750 by the directors of the French Academy in Rome, but it was exceptional to paint on a large scale. This is not

to say that Ducros diverged entirely from academic tradition: he did leave two spaces for figures which were probably added later in the studio.

29   Vue de la Vallée de la Riche
View of the Ariccia valley

Hand-coloured outline etching, J HONIG & ZOONEN paper
$12\frac{1}{2} \times 16\frac{3}{4}$ in (31·8 × 42·4 cm) sheet size
$9\frac{3}{8} \times 13\frac{5}{8}$ in (23·9 × 34·5 cm) image size

Inscribed (engraved letters): *Vue de la Vallée de la Riche* (centre); *Du Cros pin.* (b.l.)
Provenance: Purchased 1932
Literature: Meusel, *Miscellaneen*, 1787, pp 68–70; Herrmann, 1968, p 401; Chessex, 1982, pp 62–63
Related works: — *Vue d'Ariccia*, water-colour (51 × 77·5 cm), dated 1784, formerly William Spooner Collection and Bequest (fig D)
— Copperplate at the Calcografia di Roma (Istituto Nazionale per la Grafica)

Lausanne, MCBA (Inv. E-226)

Ariccia, a small town in the Colli Albani, was visited by travellers on the Grand Tour on their way to Lakes Albano and Nemi. It was 'notable for its fine position and for the rotunda built there by Bernini in his elegant manner. Here the path turns once again, crossing a wood of oaks, always cool and shady even at the burning hour of noon, and leads to the shores of Lake Albano'.[1]

The original water-colour of 1784 on which this etching is based was until recently in the collection of William Spooner (fig D). The etcher added some figures, notably the man drawing in the open air.

Ducros' collaboration with Raffaele Morghen may be dated between 1784 and 1786, and no doubt arose through his being the pupil and

fig. D
Ducros,
Vue d'Ariccia, formerly
William Spooner
Collection.

son-in-law of Ducros' associate, Giovanni Volpato, whose daughter Domenica he had married in 1782.[2]

The original copperplates of their etchings, after letters, carry the following statement and titles: 'Du Cros pin/Raf. Morghen inc./Roma presso la calcografia Camerale'.

1. *Vüe de la Vallée de la Riche*
2. *La Cascatelle de Tyvoly*
3. *La Cascade de Terny* (Ducros' name is not engraved)
4. *Le Tombeau des Horaces et des Curias a Albano*
5. *La grotte de Palazzuolo sur le Lac d'Albano*
6. *La grotte de Neptune à Tyvoly* (see cat no 56)
7. *Le Lac d'Albano*
8. *Les Marais Pontins* (see cat no 55)

These small hand-coloured outline etchings exist in several states: a set before letters, isolated prints where only the title is engraved and not the artist's name, while some carry only Ducros' name (as here) or only Morghen's.

[1] Meyer in Chevalier, op cit, p 152.
[2] AV, S. Lorenzo, Liber matrimoniorum, 10.2.1782; and the marriage certificate: Notaio Clementi, 1782, fol 634–635.

29

NAPLES AND SOUTHERN ITALY

30 Vue générale de Pouzzoles
General view of Pozzuoli

Pen and black ink, water-colour, papers laid down on canvas
$27\frac{1}{8} \times 39$ in (69×99 cm)

Inscribed (on the stone on the left, being read by a child): *Du Cr..*
Provenance: See no 1
Literature: Agassiz, 1927, p 38

Lausanne, MCBA (Inv. D-797)

The town of Pozzuoli is situated on the roads which open between the promontory of Posillipo and Capo Miseno, at the heart of the volcanic Campi Flegrei.

An old label on the back of the picture reads *Castellamare*; however, among the trees on the right of the composition can be seen the three columns of the Temple of Jupiter Serapis at Pozzuoli (see cat no 31), and, higher up, the battlements of the medieval tower which overlooks it.[1] The contrast between the warm tones of the foreground with its figures and the cool bluish tones of the background is characteristic of Ducros' style between 1793 and 1799.

[1] This tower can also be seen in the engraving of the *Temple de Sérapis* by Desprez and Piranesi (reproduced in Wollin, 1933, fig 56).

30

31 Temple de Jupiter Sérapis à Pouzzoles
Temple of Jupiter Serapis at Pozzuoli

Water-colour, papers laid down on canvas
$29 \times 43\frac{1}{8}$ in ($73 \cdot 5 \times 109 \cdot 5$ cm)

Inscribed (b.l. in pencil, barely legible): *Il y Bard…e*
Provenance: See no 1
Related works: —Drawing in pen, pencil and blue wash on JAMES WHATMAN TURKEY MILL KENT 1781 paper (67×105 cm), Lausanne (MCBA)

31

colour plate IV

32

colour plate V

33

34

Lausanne, MCBA (Inv. D-811)

These ruins were believed to be the remains of a Temple of Jupiter Serapis but are in fact of a Roman public market (*macellum*), badly damaged by changing water levels. The site has three very characteristic columns without capitals, and was much admired, and often painted, by artists including Volaire, Piranesi and Houel. Desprez painted a fine water-colour of it in 1780 (Nationalmuseum, Stockholm), which was etched by Piranesi. The viewpoint is a little higher than Ducros', but the composition is similar with the columns on the left, column shafts lying in the foreground, and the battlements of the tower outlined against the sky. This composition can also be found in a more idealized form on the engraving after a drawing by P A Pâris for Saint-Non's *Voyage pittoresque*.

Ducros collaborated with Desprez and Piranesi around 1781–83, and probably adapted this water-colour from a contemporary sketch (a preparatory sketch without figures is watermarked 1781). At his business in the Strada della Croce he coloured and sold prints by Desprez and Piranesi (Wollin, 1933, pp 32–33). Ducros' studio collection in Lausanne contains numerous drawings after Desprez and a squared reduction in pen (29·7 × 47·7 cm) after the engraving *Temple de Sérapis* by Piranesi and Desprez.

During his time in Naples Ducros took up sketching once again, making several views of this site from different angles, to which his assistant added the same groups of elegant figures. This painting is notable for the delicacy of the colouring and the finesse with which the reflections in the water have been depicted.

32 Intérieur de l'Amphithéâtre à Pouzzoles
Interior of the Amphitheatre at Pozzuoli

Pen and black ink, water-colour, the figures heightened in gouache, papers laid down on canvas
27 × 41¼ in (68·5 × 105 cm)

Provenance : See no 1
Literature : Agassiz, 1927, p 42

Lausanne, MCBA (Inv. D-842)

'The grandeur of the amphitheatre of Pozzuoli indicates the population of this ancient town since it was nearly as big as the Colosseum in Rome. . . . The Arena, which today is simply a garden planted with vines and poplars, is 250 feet in length. The porticoes which served as entrances, to be found beneath the tiers, exist almost in their entirety, as do the cells where the animals destined for combat were kept. . . . This edifice had two storeys, or orders, the first being built of rough blocks of lava, the upper one of *mattoni*, or bricks'.[1]

Ducros has depicted a portico on the lower level with its characteristic stone. Using one of his favourite viewpoints—looking out onto countryside through an archway, he created effects through backlighting. For the foliage in the middle distance he superimposed grey-green tones onto yellow resin (gamboge) to obtain further astonishing effects of light.

This dark grotto, illuminated by one or two bursts of light and covered in vegetation, is typical of Ducros' work during his years in

Naples. The playful style and bright colour of the picturesque figures enlivens the composition and is a feature of the work of the mysterious assistant Ducros employed at this time.

[1]   Jean Claude Richard de Saint-Non, *Voyage pittoresque ou description des royaumes de Naples et de Sicile*, Paris, 1781–6, vol II, 1782, p 179.

33   La Grotte du Pausilippe
The Grotto of Posillipo

Pen and sepia ink, water-colour,
J WHATMAN papers laid down on canvas
$31\frac{1}{8} \times 43\frac{1}{4}$ in (79 × 110 cm)

Inscribed: (on the reverse of the original canvas in brush): *Vüe de la Grotte/de Pausillippe/près de Naples*
Provenance: See no 1
Literature: Chessex, 1982, fig 8 and 1984 (2), fig p 76
Related works: —Pen drawing, squared and surrounded with a border (area within border: 29·2 × 47·8 cm), Lausanne (MCBA). An exact reduction probably made in preparation for an etching.

Lausanne, MCBA (Inv. D-822)

'Continuing my walk, I found the grotto of Posillipo, a road 500 yards long, very high, very wide, hollowed through the mountain to shorten the route from Naples to Pozzuoli. A prodigious feat of work and confidence! The road is cobbled with lava: it is the work of the Romans'.[1] The *Crypta Neapolitana* is a tunnel built by Claudius in the middle of the first century A.D., and was altered many times through the centuries, being used until 1885. This picture shows its entrance on the Naples side. It was much visited by travellers in the eighteenth century on their way to the so-called Virgil's Tomb which overlooks the entrance to the tunnel from the hillside on the left (see cat

no 35). Many artists painted the site, including Jan Blaeu, Caspar van Wittel, Hubert Robert, Joseph Wright of Derby, L-J Desprez and Francis Towne.

Ducros employed the same frontal viewpoint as Châtelet used in Saint-Non's *Voyage pittoresque* (fig E), but strengthened the monumental effect by having a very high vanishing point. The grandeur of the site is further emphasized by the very small section of sky, the small figures, the close viewpoint and the wide angle of the view. But the total effect is tempered by the picturesque nature of the figures drawn in the style of the Venetian assistant Ducros used in Naples between 1793 and 1805.

[1]   (Dupaty), *Lettres sur l'Italie en 1785*, vol I, Lausanne, 1789, p 132.

34   Temple de la Fortune à Marechiaro (Naples)
Temple of Fortune at Marechiaro, Naples

Pen and sepia ink, pencil, water-colour, the figures heightened in gouache, D & C BLAUW papers laid down on canvas
$30\frac{1}{8} \times 44\frac{5}{8}$ in (76·5 × 113·4 cm)

Provenance: See no 1
Exhibited: Lausanne, 1953, no 45; Rome, 1954, no 35; Naples, 1962, no 30 and pl X; Lausanne, 1974, no 145
Literature: Agassiz, 1927, p 43
Related works: —Etching of the same site (area within border: 17·7 × 25 cm), Lausanne (MCBA)
—View of the same site from the other side, Lausanne (MCBA)

Lausanne, MCBA (Inv. D-849)

Marechiaro is a tiny fishing village at the tip of Capo Posillipo, famous for its view of the Bay of Naples and Vesuvius. Dominique Vivant-Denon wrote of it: 'The only ruin to be found there is the stump of an ancient column in fluted

fig. E
Desmoulins after Châtelet, *La Grotte du Pausilippe*, from: Abbé de Saint-Non, *Voyage pittoresque . . . de Naples et de Sicile*, vol I, 1781.

marble with a Corinthian base: it is in front of a shapeless mass of bricks, or *mattoni*; . . . these are the remains of a Temple of *Fortune*. An inscription has been placed there in our time to remind the traveller that he is walking in the steps of a hero'.[1]

No illustration of this site accompanies the text in the *Voyage pittoresque* because the ancient remains in Marechiaro 'are in such a state of destruction that we did not think it necessary to present them here'[2]. Ducros, who between 1793 and 1799 lived in nearby Chiaja found them worthy of attention and made two large views and an etching. In this drawing the archaeological site provides the opportunity for a picturesque genre scene, as Ducros attaches more importance to the alley and the people in it than to the ruined temple. The latter is, however, drawn with great precision (compare Vivant-Denon's description) and the shadows of the foliage on the column are extremely delicate.

[1] Saint-Non, *Voyage pittoresque* vol II, 1782, p 163.
[2] Ibid.

35 Tombeau de Virgile (Pausilippe)
Virgil's Tomb, Posillipo

Water-colour, heightened with gouache, papers laid down on canvas
$33\frac{3}{4} \times 47\frac{3}{4}$ in ($85 \cdot 5 \times 121 \cdot 5$ cm)

Provenance: See no 1
Exhibited: Lausanne, 1953, no 46; Rome, 1954, no 36; Naples, 1962, no 31
Literature: Agassiz, 1927, p 42

fig. F
Volpato after Nicole,
Sepolcro di Virgilio,
from: *Avanzi delle
Antichità esistenti a
Pozzuoli*, 1768.

Lausanne, MCBA (Inv. D-854)

'There is not a single foreigner or traveller arriving in Naples who does not count among his priorities a visit to Virgil's Tomb, there to render homage to the shade of this famous man; although, as we have already stated, it is somewhat uncertain that the little ruined monument given this name was ever truly the tomb of this poet'.[1]

To paraphrase Vivant-Denon, one could say that this classic site was one of the first views a foreign artist would sketch on arriving in Naples. Vernet, Volaire, Robert, and Nicole, not to mention the Italians Fabris, Bonavia and Dominici, drew and painted it many times. To compare Ducros' view to other depictions of the site (such as the engraving of 1768 by Volpato after a drawing by Nicole, fig F) is to be struck by the originality of Ducros' composition. This can be seen in the splendid treatment of the different levels of space, the entrance to the *Crypta Neapolitana* (see cat no 33) in the middle distance below the tomb, and in the distant bluish vista with the Chiaja area and the Castel Sant'Elmo minutely depicted.

The contrast between the warm tones of the vegetation and rocks in the foreground and the cool tones of the buildings of Naples and the pines on the hill to the left increases the immediacy of the site. The figures, although stereotyped,[2] give rhythm to the composition. The light colour of their clothes was obtained by leaving the paper bare and applying white gouache highlights.

[1] Saint-Non, *Voyage pittoresque* vol I, 1781, p 83.
[2] The group on the left can be found in a view of Malta (see cat no 45), while the figures in the centre can be found in a later painting, where they also come out of a grotto (see cat no 50).

36 Vue Idéalisée du Pausilippe
An idealized view of Posillipo

Pen and black ink, water-colour, the figures heightened in gouache, D & C BLAUW paper laid down on canvas
$29\frac{1}{2} \times 45\frac{1}{4}$ in (75×115 cm)

Inscribed (in brush on the reverse of the original canvas): *Veduta del Posilippo/verso Napoli*
Provenance: See no 1
Exhibited: Lausanne, 1953, no 42 and fig; Rome, 1954, no 33
Literature: Agassiz, 1927, p 42; Logoz, 1956, p 7 and fig
Related works: —*Posilippo visto da Palazzo Donn'Anna*, water-colour (67×104 cm), Museo Nazionale di San Martino, Naples, (fig G)

Lausanne, MCBA (Inv. D-810)

We know that Ducros' views, for all their precision of detail, are not objective in the sense in which the word has been used since the invention of photography. He had numerous methods of altering the real appearance of a scene, such as modifying the proportions of buildings, stretching space, and using multiple viewpoints. In this water-colour he goes even further, making us doubt the accuracy of his inscriptions. Although he wrote by hand on the reverse of the canvas *Veduta del Posilippo*, this is in fact a montage, its starting point being an exact view of Posillipo from the Palazzo Donn'Anna, a work formerly at Caserta, now at the Museo di San Martino, Naples (fig G). For the Naples painting Ducros placed himself under one of the arcades which support the palace and, using one of his favourite devices, depicted the sunlit shore of Posillipo and the Riviera di Chiaja rising up in the background beyond the dark archway. In the Lausanne water-colour the dark mass of the arch is absent; instead an imaginary group of trees forms a partial substitute for the archway. Then, above the shores of Posillipo he placed a second tier of steep hills, crowning the whole with the characteristic silhouette of the Castel Sant'Elmo. The Riviera di Chiaja in the background becomes Naples dominated by Vesuvius. This is, then, a landscape of real elements arranged according to the painter's imagination.

This landscape and the one at Naples are also of great interest as they depict the shoreline between Mergellina and the Palazzo Donn'Anna with such great precision that we can distinguish Sir William Hamilton's mysterious Villa Emma with its characteristic semi-circular terrace. A water-colour (now lost) by William Pars was one of the few documents of the layout of Hamilton's villa at Posillipo, but showed it from the other side with the Palazzo Donn'Anna in the background.[1] This is another souvenir of the years 1794–95 recalling the famous 'Casino di Posilippo' where so many famous people visited Sir William Hamilton.

[1]   Carlo Knight 'I luoghi di delizie di William Hamilton' *Napoli Nobilissima* XX (1981) pp 180–3, fig 4.

37   Eruption du Vésuve et naufrage
Shipwreck with the Eruption of Vesuvius

Water-colour, heightened with gouache and oil, remains of varnish, papers laid down on canvas
$40\frac{1}{2} \times 28\frac{5}{8}$ in (103 × 72·7 cm)

Provenance: See no 1
Exhibited: Lausanne, 1953, no 43

35

colour plate IX

36

fig. G
Ducros, *Posilippo visto da Palazzo Donn'Anna*, Museo Nazionale di San Martino, Naples.

37

Related works: —Identical view of the same dimensions, Lausanne (MCBA)
—Two drawings in pen and pencil (97 × 75 cm), Lausanne (MCBA)

Lausanne, MCBA (Inv. D-819)

Only two examples of this kind of shipwreck, conceived in the manner of Vernet, are known to exist among Ducros' works. Little is known about his years in Naples, but it seems likely that after seeing the dramatic views of Vesuvius by P-J Volaire and Michael Wutky he wanted to show that water-colour could compete with oil painting. He was not completely successful and must have realized this when he wrote to Sir Richard Colt Hoare from Malta in 1800: 'They snatched Vesuvius from me over my shoulder' (see Appendix 1). Towards the end of his career in Italy Ducros was less at ease treating foaming waves and clouds of cinders from the volcano than he had been during his Roman years when he painted cascades with their clouds of fine spray.

38

38 Chantier naval à Castellammare di Stabia
Shipyard at Castellammare di Stabia

Pen and black ink, water-colour, heightened with gouache and oil, papers laid down canvas
$29\frac{7}{8} \times 42\frac{7}{8}$ in (76 × 109 cm)

Provenance: See no 1
Literature: Gerning, 1802, Part II; Agassiz, 1927, p 38

Lausanne, MCBA (Inv. D-821)

The shipyards at Castellammare on the bay of Naples between Pompeii and Sorrento were founded by Ferdinand IV of the Bourbons in 1783, very near the *Antiche Terme Stabiane.* When Ducros settled in Naples in 1793 the shipyards were still new and fully active. John Francis Edward Acton (1736–1811) had been put in charge of the reorganisation of the Neapolitan fleet in 1778 and had made a significant contribution to developing the shipyards. He was made Prime Minister in 1790 and played an important rôle in the Kingdom of Naples' diplomatic dealings with England; he became a baronet in 1791.
Around 1794–96 Acton bought four large water-colours from Ducros portraying various aspects of the naval shipyards (see cat nos 77–9). He had already assembled a fine collection in his Naples residence, including paintings by Simon Denis and J P Hackert. J I Gerning also reports that Ducros painted for him 'a room full of varnished gouaches; particularly superb among these is the launching of a warship against a background of the chestnut-covered slopes of Castellammare, in the presence of the royal family and a large crowd' (Gerning, 1802). Gerning must have made this visit before 1798, since in December of that year Acton had to leave Naples for Sicily with the court.
The Lausanne painting depicts the launching of the warship *Archimedes* in the presence of the royal family who are not in view although the rear part of their dais can be seen flanked by four flags. The picture may be compared to a view by J P Hackert showing the launching of the *Parthenope* in 1786 (fig H), the first in a series of *Ports of the Kingdom of the Two Sicilies* commissioned from the German painter by Ferdinand IV along the lines of C J Vernet's *Ports of France.* Ducros had been in competition with Hackert in Rome and was no doubt keen to show that he could keep up with the best in Naples as well. The view from above, the multiple vanishing points and the disproportion of the various elements of the composition give the painting an almost fantastic quality, distinguishing it from Hackert's cool, precise view.

39 Temple de Mercure à Baia
Temple of Mercury, Baia

Water-colour, the figures heightened in gouache, D & C BLAUW paper laid down on canvas
$26\frac{1}{2} \times 41\frac{1}{8}$ in (67·5 × 104 cm)

Provenance: See no 1
Literature: Agassiz, 1927, p 42; Chessex, 1984 (2), fig p 77

Lausanne, MCBA (Inv. D-834)

The Temple of Mercury is one of the three ruined buildings of the antique baths at Baia

IL CANTIERE DI CASTEL LAMMARE DI STABIA

fig. H G after P Hackert, *Il cantiere di Castellammare di Stabia*, Bibliothèque Nationale, Paris.

fig. I Volpato after Natali, *Tempio di Mercurio, Baia*, from: *Avanzi delle Antichità esistenti a Pozzuoli*, 1768.

39

which were flooded after violent earthquakes in the area. Although difficult to reach, the baths were popular with travellers on the Grand Tour. 'The water remaining there blocks the avenues, preventing all access were it not for the *Lazaroni*, the peasants of the region, who offer the use of their shoulders, going up to their waists in water to carry you there.'[1]

The site was often depicted in prints and drawings. Ducros' predecessors only drew part of the vault, (see for example C-L Clérisseau in *Piranése et les Francais*, Rome, Dijon and Paris, 1976, fig 39), or they positioned themselves further back beneath the arcades, as in Natali's picture engraved by Volpato in 1768 (see fig I). Ducros chose to place himself directly beneath the vault and instead of a view from the side painted a grandiose view of the chamber as if through a wide-angle lens. He even left out the oblique shafts of light from openings in the roof which his predecessors, and he himself, usually favoured. Instead, Ducros has a circle of light fall on the lower right-hand side of the vault and includes the reflection of a section of sky in the water.

The various groups of figures, not painted to scale, further emphasize the immense size of the chamber, and provide some indication of the attitudes of travellers on the Grand Tour and their contact with local inhabitants.

[1] Saint-Non, *Voyage pittoresque* vol. II, 1782, p 215

40
colour plate VIII

40 Vue des Temples de Paestum
View of the Temples at Paestum

Water-colour and grey wash, heightened with gouache and oil, the figures in pen and sepia ink, D & C BLAUW papers laid down on canvas
29⅞ × 44⅛ in (76 × 112 cm)

Inscribed (in brush on the reverse of the original canvas): *Les 3 Temples de Pestum*
Provenance: See no 1
Exhibited: Lausanne, 1953, no 39; Rome, 1954, no 31
Literature: Agassiz, 1927, p 83; *Gazette des Beaux-Arts*, April 1982, chronicle, fig p 22
Related works: —View of the same site, water-colour (77 × 114 cm), private collection, Geneva (exhibited Geneva, 1789, no 27)
—Pen drawing with border (29·7 × 46·7 cm), preparation for etching, Lausanne (MCBA)
—Various proofs and counter-proofs of an outline etching (53 × 74 cm), with different figures, Lausanne (MCBA)

Lausanne, MCBA (Inv. D-796)

The temples at Paestum were rediscovered in the middle of the eighteenth century and the first publications on these Doric ruins appeared between 1764 and 1784.[1] Many travellers on their way to Sicily or Greece at this time passed the Gulf of Salerno without stopping, and the Dutch group with which Ducros travelled in 1778 took the inland route from Naples to the Adriatic coast, similarly bypassing Paestum. Ducros is not known to have visited the site at a later date. Although certain drawings in Lausanne would seem to suggest that he did visit Paestum, he kept remarkably close to the compositional schemes found in nearly all contemporary publications. Giovanni Volpato collaborated with P A Paoli on *Rovine della Città di Pesto detta Posidonia*, a collection of views of archaeological sites published in Rome in 1784, and Ducros may have based his water-colours on such prints. Although this oblique view of the three temples is one of the first large-scale water-colours of the site, in composition it is quite traditional. 1789 is the *terminus ante quem* for this painting, as Ducros exhibited an identical view at the Salon de la Société des Arts in Geneva that year (private collection, Geneva).

[1] S. Lang, 'The Early Publications of the Temples at Paestum', *Journal of the Warburg and Courtauld Institutes* XIII (1950) pp 48–64.

41 Orage nocturne à Cefalù
Storm at night, Cefalù

Water-colour, gouache and oil, papers laid down on canvas
37¾ × 29⅛ in (96 × 74 cm)

Inscribed (in brush on the reverse of the original canvas): *Orage nocturne a Ceffalou*
Provenance: See no 1
Exhibited: Lausanne, 1953, no 60 and fig; Rome, 1954, no 42; Stockholm, 1982, no 175
Literature: Agassiz, 1927, p 44; Castelnuovo, 1976, fig p 113; F. Zeri *Storia d'Italia*, II/2, Turin, 1976, fig 96; Briganti, 1977, fig 35; *Museen der Schweiz*, Zurich, 1983, fig p 170; Chessex, 1984 (2), pl p 78

Lausanne, MCBA (Inv. D-812)

41

42

opposite:
colour plate XII

In the present century this has become one of
Ducros' best known works due to its frequent
use as an example of the emergence of
imagination and fantasy in art around 1800. But
it is the least documented, as no relevant
sketches, drawings or contemporary writings
exist. Judging by the technique and style, it must
date from the painter's final period, between
1799 and 1806, as it brings to a climax the
sublime elements already seen in the water-
colours of Naples and Malta, notably the
eruptions in the former and the skies in the
latter. The subject-matter is indebted to
seventeenth century sources such as Gaspard
Dughet and Salvator Rosa, but here the
unchained forces of nature take precedence over
any picturesque or anecdotal element, becoming
the principal motif of the painting. In this way
Ducros anticipates the development of this
theme in the first quarter of the nineteenth
century, in the landscapes of Théodore Gudin,
Thomas Girtin, John Constable and John
Martin.

42   Vue de Messine après le tremblement de terre de 1783
View of Messina after the Earthquake of 1783

Pen and black ink, water-colour,
D & C BLAUW paper laid down on canvas
$26\frac{3}{8} \times 40\frac{1}{8}$ in (67×102 cm)

Inscribed (in pen on the reverse): *129. Vue de
Messine après le tremblement de terre*
Provenance: See no 1

Lausanne, MCBA (Inv. D-84/59)

On his second trip to Sicily, around 1788–89,
Ducros made numerous drawings for a planned
series of prints to be published in collaboration
with Pier Paolo Montagnani. Another view of
Messina by Ducros, depicting the destroyed
Palazzata (water-colour, $46·5 \times 92$ cm, Geneva
art market, April 1983) is a large composition
with a stormy sky and figures. In contrast to the
drama of that view, the one from Lausanne is

peaceful, showing desolate deserted houses.
Travellers reported how the effects of the
earthquake were still evident several years after
the disaster. Goethe (13th May 1787) tells how
'this row of houses, once magnificent, now has
a horribly broken and riddled appearance: for
the blue sky can be seen through nearly all the
windows; the whole interior, which was once
lived in, has collapsed'.[1] In the summer of 1788
a Swiss traveller made a similar comment about
the destruction of the town.[2]
Confronted with this ruined town, Ducros
painted a surprisingly spontaneous and fresh
picture no doubt intending to use it later in a
larger composition.

[1]   J. W. Goethe, *Italienische Reise*, in *Goethes Werke*, Vol
11, Hamburg, 1954.
[2]   Karl U. Salis von Marschlins, 'Beschreibung einer Reise
in Sicilien in Briefen', *Beiträge zur natürlichen und
ökonomischen Kenntnis des Königreichs beider Sicilien*, Vol 1,
Zürich, 1790, p 271.

MALTA

43   Vue de Grand Port de la Valette
View of Grand Harbour, Valletta

Pen and black ink, water-colour, heightened
with gouache, papers laid down on canvas
$30\frac{7}{8} \times 50\frac{1}{4}$ in ($78·5 \times 127·5$ cm)

Inscribed (in brush on the reverse of the original
canvas): *Malta/dalla parte verso l'ingresso del
Porto/presa dalla Batteria di Dukens*
Provenance: See no 1
Exhibited: Lausanne, 1953, no 54; Rome, 1954,
no 38

43

Literature: Agassiz, 1927, p 45; *ILN*, 1946
Related works: —Virtually identical view, water-colour and oil (85·5 × 132 cm), National Museum of Fine Arts, Valletta, probably commissioned by Brigadier-General Thomas Graham, later Lord Lynedoch, in 1800

Lausanne, MCBA (Inv. D-802)

This view is taken from a point below the Upper Barracca which overlooks the Marina Gate of Grand Harbour at Valletta, Malta, and shows some English boats moored there (see cat no 48).
Ducros stayed in Malta from November 1800 to May 1801 and made numerous views of Valletta, which had only recently been taken from Napoleon's troops by the English, under the command of Ducros' patron, Brigadier-General Graham. Ducros also intended to engrave a series of views of Malta, 'boulevards de la Puissance Britannique' as he described them in a letter to Sir Richard Colt Hoare (see Appendix 1). The collections in Lausanne (MCBA) include twenty-five large water-colour views of the island and about fifty drawings.
The view of the harbour is very precise, with the houses of Valletta, the Bastion of St. Barbara with its look-out tower, the characteristic arcades of the Lower Barracca, and, closing off the harbour in the background, Fort Ricasoli (fig K). This is not to say that Ducros did not add his own touches to the composition: the Fort Sant' Angelo on the extreme right has been displaced to achieve a balanced effect. It would, in fact, be out of sight on the right but for the painter's 'wide-angle' view.
The slightly larger painting at the National Museum of Fine Arts in Malta is identical in subject to the one in Lausanne, but its untroubled sky casts fewer contrasts between light and shadow over the city. The painting has

also suffered from the passage of time, due to the mixed media (water-colour, gouache, oil and varnish) of which Ducros made particular use towards the end of his life.

44 Fontaine de Neptune et Marché aux Poissons à la Valette
Fountain of Neptune and Fish Market at Valletta

Pen and black ink, water-colour, heightened with gouache, D & C BLAUW papers laid down on canvas
33 × 52 in (83·7 × 132 cm)

Inscribed (in brush on the reverse of the original canvas): *Gran Veduta/dal Porto Carbone/dietro alla fontana*
Provenance: See no 1
Exhibited: Lausanne, 1953, no 56 and fig; Rome, 1954, no 40 and fig
Literature: Agassiz, 1927, p 45
Related works: —Virtually identical view, water-colour and oil, National Museum of Fine Arts, Valletta (see cat no 43)
—Water-colour and oil (67·5 × 104 cm), same site from a different angle, Lausanne (MCBA)
—Several preparatory drawings and tracings, Lausanne (MCBA)

Lausanne, MCBA (Inv. D-805)

The old fish market (destroyed in the last war) and the Fountain of Neptune (statue now in the courtyard of the Grand Masters' Palace) are here depicted in minute detail in a scene enlivened by numerous figures. The market was actually held beneath the Bastion of St. Barbara. Beyond the fountain are the quays of Grand Harbour and the arcades of the Lower Barracca, with Fort Ricasoli on the right behind

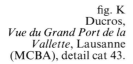

fig. K
Ducros,
Vue du Grand Port de la Vallette, Lausanne (MCBA), detail cat 43.

merchant ships carrying coal (in a version of this picture in Malta the prow of the boat on the extreme right carries the inscription: 'Carbone del.ᵃ Spiagia Romana').
Although it is unfinished (particularly in the lower left-hand corner), this water-colour is unusually powerful, and shows what Sir Richard Colt Hoare meant when he said of Ducros: 'His work proved the force, as well as the consequence that could be given to the unsubstantial body of water-colours'.[1]

[1] Colt Hoare, 1822, p 83.

44

colour plate XI

45   Vue de Grand Port de la Valette
View of Grand Harbour, Valletta

Pen and black ink, water-colour, heightened with gouache, D & C BLAUW and J WHATMAN papers laid down on canvas
$34\frac{5}{8} \times 62\frac{3}{4}$ in (88 × 159·5 cm)

Provenance: See no 1
Literature: Agassiz, 1927, p 46
Related works: —Pen and pencil drawing on tracing paper (84 × 164 cm), Lausanne (MCBA)
—Virtually identical view, water-colour and oil (102·5 × 164 cm), National Museum of Fine Arts, Valletta (cat no 43).

Lausanne, MCBA (Inv. D-860)

This view from the Bastion of St. James down onto Grand Harbour shows a wing of the Upper Barracca on the heights to the left and, opposite, the 'Three Cities': Vittoriosa and part of the Fort Sant' Angelo on the left, Cospicua at the back of the bay and Senglea on the right. The whole view is an accurate panorama of the port of Valletta.
The version in Valletta has slightly different figures, and the ships are surrounded by cannon smoke. The couple with a child on the left of the picture are taken directly from an earlier painting (see cat no 35).

45

colour plate X

46   Pavillon du Jardin des Grands-Maîtres à la Valette
Pavilion in the Grand Master's Garden, Valletta

Pen and black ink, water-colour, heightened with gouache, papers laid down on canvas
$30\frac{3}{4} \times 46\frac{1}{2}$ in (78 × 118 cm)

Inscribed (in brush on the reverse of the original canvas): *Burascha dietro alla Dogana*; crossed out above: *Il temporale della Valle di Terny/di Rovigliano per Mr Bernis*
Provenance: See no 1
Exhibited: Lausanne, 1953, no 53
Literature: Agassiz, 1927, p 39
Related works: —Various drawings and sketches on tracing paper of the same site, and two drawings on D & C BLAUW paper, Lausanne (MCBA)

Lausanne, MCBA (Inv. D-795)

This painting includes a number of landmarks already discussed in the previous entries, most notably the Fountain of Neptune and the Bastion of St. Barbara. To get a better idea of the position of the Pavilion by the counterfort in the Grand Masters' Garden, compare the view of the same site from a distance which

46

47

This part of Valletta was the main entrance to the city when Ducros painted it but was completely demolished in 1964. Although unfinished, this water-colour admirably conveys the atmosphere of Malta, with its tall houses brightened by numerous different coloured loggias (*galleriji*). The sketch-like nature of the picture allows us to appreciate the delicacy of Ducros' colouring, before any work was done at the studio, in a subtle harmony of pinks, yellows and blues. Unfinished drawings may appeal to the late twentieth-century spectator with a charm not often found in finished paintings, but it is worth remembering that incomplete works like this were not intended for public display.

48 Porte de la Marine à la Valette
The Marina Gate, Valletta

Pen and sepia ink, water-colour, heightened with gouache and oil, papers laid down on canvas
$32 \times 48\frac{1}{2}$ in (81 × 123 cm)

Inscribed (in brush on the reverse of the original canvas): *Vue extérieure de la/Porte de la Marine/du petit escalier Ville Valette Malthe*
Provenance: See no 1
Related works: —Water-colour, gouache and oil (76 × 120 cm), Lausanne (MCBA)
—Water-colour, gouache and oil (110·5 × 162 cm), Lausanne (MCBA)
—Pen and pencil drawing J WHATMAN paper (80 × 118 cm), inscribed: *lucido della scala della Porta della Marina* and a Cyrillic inscription, Lausanne (MCBA)

Lausanne, MCBA (Inv. D-830)

This view from the foot of the Bastion of St. Barbara at the level of Grand Harbour quay looks towards the Upper Barracca in exactly the opposite direction from the *View of Grand Harbour* (cat no 43). A reference point is the open wooden gate in both drawings, seen from opposite sides.

Ducros painted twenty-two years earlier on his trip to the Kingdom of the Two Sicilies and to Malta (cat no 52).
The two inscriptions on the reverse of the original canvas are worth noting. We should not be surprised that Ducros reused canvases for mounting his paper as he had to watch his finances from 1799. But it is interesting that 'Mr Bernis' is named as having commissioned a version of *Storm in the Valley of Terni*, since it was not otherwise known that Ducros had painted for Cardinal de Bernis, French Ambassador to Rome, a man who played an important role in the artistic life of the 1780s.

47 La Porte Royale à la Valette
The Porta Reale, Valletta

Pen and black ink, water-colour, the figures heightened with gouache, D & C BLAUW papers laid down on canvas
$26\frac{1}{2} \times 43\frac{1}{2}$ in (67·5 × 110·3 cm)

Provenance: See no 1
Exhibited: Lausanne, 1953, no 58 and fig; Rome, 1954 and fig
Literature: Agassiz, 1927, p 46
Related works: —Three pen drawings of the same site (67 × 103 cm), squared for transfer, Lausanne (MCBA)

Lausanne, MCBA (Inv. D-833)

49 Vue du Fort St Ange à la Valette
View of the Fort Sant' Angelo, Valletta

Pen and sepia ink, water-colour, heightened with gouache, papers laid down on canvas
$30\frac{1}{2} \times 42\frac{1}{4}$ in (77·5 × 107·5 cm)

Provenance: See no 1
Literature: Agassiz, 1927, p 39 (as *Porte de la Marine*); Chessex, 1984 (2), fig p 70
Related works: —Water-colour with different lighting and alterations in the figures (76·2 × 106·5 cm), Lausanne (MCBA)
—Two pen drawings (same dimensions), Lausanne (MCBA)
—Etching inscribed *Luigi du Cros dipinse* (b.l.), (area within border 39·6 × 56 cm), Lausanne (MCBA)

Lausanne, MCBA (Inv. D-820)

Using one of his favourite devices, Ducros represented the Fort Sant' Angelo in the middle distance through the customs arch just below the Upper Barracca. This is the only view of Valletta known to have been etched by Ducros. He employed a traditional process bearing no

48

relation to the outline-etchings he made with Volpato in Rome.

50 Grotte des Pages à Malte
Grotte des Pages, Malta

Water-colour and oil, papers laid down on canvas
34 × 47¾ in (86·5 × 121·5 cm)

Provenance: See no 1
Literature: Guattani, 1807, pp72–73; Fernow, 1809, pp 37–38; Agassiz, 1927, p 38; Hardtwig, 1978, pp 65–68; Chessex, 1982, p 67
Related works: —Oil on canvas (92 × 123·5 cm), Neue Pinakothek, Munich
—Water-colour and oil (89·5 × 120·5 cm), Lausanne (MCBA)
—Pen drawing, J WHATMAN 1801 paper (78 × 125 cm), Lausanne (MCBA).
—Pen and wash drawing, J WHATMAN 1797 and HAYES & WISE 1799 papers (92 × 132·5 cm), Lausanne (MCBA)
—Pen and pencil drawing, JAN KOOL papers (93 × 125 cm), Lausanne (MCBA)

Lausanne, MCBA (Inv. D-825)

Fort Ricasoli, which closes off the Grand Harbour of Valletta, is seen in the distance. The brewing storm, dark grotto and the setting sun are combined to dramatic effect.
This is a copy of the painting bought from Ducros in Rome in 1806 by Friedrich von Sachsen-Gotha and described thus by Guattani: 'The pen is powerless to describe the power and effect with which Monsieur Du Cros' brushes have depicted the terror of this huge grotto opening onto the exterior, and whose entrance is like an optical tube in enabling us to discover the view of the sea and Fort' (*Memorie*, II, 1807). This is one of the few existing paintings by Ducros in which oil dominates over water-colour. The broad strokes of the threatening sky herald the age of Romantic landscape painting.

49

50

51   Vue de Tarente
View of Taranto

Water-colour over pencil, ink border,
J HONIG & ZOONEN paper
7⅛ × 20¾ in (18·2 × 52·8 cm)

Inscribed (in ink on reverse): *No 104 Vue de la
Citadelle de Tarente*

*Dessins/de mon voyage dans les Deux Siciles/et/à
Malte/1778/Louis Ducros fecit/*, vol I, fol 86,
no 104

Provenance: Commissioned by Nicolas Ten
Hove on his trip to the South in 1778.
Rijksprentenkabinet since 1948
Literature: J. W. Niemeijer, 'Het reisverhaal
van W. C. Dierkens in het Rijksprentenkabinet',
Nederlands Kunsthistorisch Jaarboek 32, (1981),
pp 227–230; Chessex, 1984, (1) p 431; Chessex,
1984, (2) pp 70–71; J. W. Niemeijer, 'Een Grand
Tour in beeld. Vier Hagenaars in 1778 met een
Zwitserse vedutenkenaar op reis door Italië'.
Herinneringen aan Italië, Frans Halsmuseum,
Haarlem; Noordbrabants Museum,
S' Hertogenbosch; Kasteel Het Nijenhuis,
Heino, 1984, pp 63–67.

Rijksprentenkabinet, Amsterdam

52   Vue du Port de la Valette (Malte)
View of Valletta Harbour, Malta

Water-colour over pencil and ink, ink border,
J HONIG & ZOONEN paper
13¼ × 20¾ in (33·8 × 52·8 cm)

Inscribed (in ink on reverse): *No 204 Pavillon di
jardin du Grand-Maître, en face du port des
Galères à Malthe, suite des nos 202 & 203*

Dessins/de mon voyage . . ., vol.II, fol 88, no 204
(see cat no 51)

Rijksprentenkabinet, Amsterdam

53   Temple d'Hercule à Agrigente
Temple of Hercules at Agrigento

Water-colour, pen and ink, ink border
8 × 12⅛ in (20·5 × 30·7 cm)

Inscribed (on reverse): *No 250 Débris du Temple
d'Hercule dans l'enceinte de l'ancien Agrigentum*

Dessins/de mon voyage . . ., vol III, fol 45,
no 250 (see cat no 51)

Rijksprentenkabinet, Amsterdam

As a young painter in Rome, Ducros was
engaged early in 1778 to accompany Nicolas
Ten Hove of The Hague on a trip to southern
Italy. On 10th April 1778 a group formed by
Ten Hove, his cousin W C Dierkens and his
friends N Thornbury and W van Nieuwerkerke,
all respected members of The Hague society, left
Rome for Naples. Ducros was put to work
almost immediately. The carriage broke an axle
almost as soon as they set off, and as Dierkens
says in the manuscript of his journal: 'This
forced us to stop and gave Mr Ducros (the
painter accompanying Ten Hove) the
opportunity to make several pretty drawings of
antiquities and of the fine views on the road'.[1]
They took the Via Appia and arrived in Naples,
where they were received at Sir William
Hamilton's home, and then visited southern
Italy, Sicily (in May), Malta (June), Sicily once
more, and finally on 16th July 1778 left Palermo
for Naples in a French brigantine.
Ten Hove pasted some three hundred drawings
by Ducros into three folio volumes. They show
a great diversity of format and technique and
are a reliable source of information about
physical conditions for travellers on the Grand
Tour (see Niemeijer, 1984, p 66). They are also
accurate documents of famous and less well-
known places in southern Italy.
After the middle of the eighteenth century, in
particular following the publication of works on
Sicily by Baron von Riedesel and Sir William
Hamilton,[2] there had been a shift in interest

51

from Rome to Sicily, mixing the traditions of the Grand Tour with those of the archaeological campaigns.[3] Between 1776 and 1778 enthusiasts, experts and artists of all nationalities began to converge on the South. Richard Payne Knight made his 'Expedition into Sicily' with Charles Gore and J P Hackert exactly a year before Ten Hove's party (from 12th April to July, 1777).[4] A French team of artists and architects led by Dominique Vivant-Denon was in the area at the same time as Ten Hove and Ducros. The years 1776–79 also saw Jean-Pierre Houel's trip to the South, and his sketches were used for aquatints in his *Voyage pittoresque des isles de Sicile, de Lipari et de Malte* (1783–87). The various groups came into contact[5] and there are many coinciding views from artists such as Ducros, Houel, Desprez and C L Châtelet.

These water-colours, wash drawings and sketches are the first dated and documented works by Ducros, and show the considerable skill he acquired in Switzerland and on trips in the countryside around Geneva. Although quality varies among these hundreds of drawings many have great freshness and compositional sensitivity. This is especially true of this water-colour in which the foreground tree partially covers the Doric column, suggesting both three-dimensionality and the vegetation actually growing over the ruined temple.

A dozen drawings are missing from the three folio volumes in the Rijksprentenkabinet. It is possible, though not at all certain, that they were more valuable than the others and were removed by Ten Hove or his descendents and then framed. Notable similarities in style, technique and size exist between the *View of the Harbour at Pozzuoli* of 1778 at the Whitworth Art Gallery (cat no 63) and the drawings in the first Amsterdam volume. As in the case of some of the drawings at Lausanne,[6] the marking on the upper right of cat no 63 suggests that this is probably a sketch that the painter wanted to take up again or complete at a later stage.

1   Fol 79; the manuscript of the journal is at the Rijksprentenkabinet, Amsterdam.
2   J. H. von Riedesel, *Reise durch Sizilien und Grossgriechenland* (1767), Zurich, 1771. English edition, London, 1773; French edition with *Voyage au Mont Ethna* by Hamilton as appendix, Lausanne, 1773.
3   Cesare di Seta, 'L'Italia nello specchio del Grand Tour', *Storia d'Italia*, Annali 5, Turin, 1982, pp 227–253.
4   Claudia Stumpf, 'The Expedition into Sicily', *The Arrogant Connoisseur: Richard Payne Knight, 1751–1824*, Manchester, 1982, pp 19–31.
5   Dominique Vivant-Denon records the circumstances in which they met the Dutch party near Brindisi at the end of April, 1778 in Saint-Non's *Voyage Pittoresque ou description des royaumes de Naples et de Sicile*, Paris, 1781–86, vol III, chap 3, p 52.
6   For example the *Théâtre de Syracuse* (Inv. D-788), the uncoloured drawing of the right-hand part of a large water-colour in Amsterdam (vol II, fol 83), or the *Intérieur d'une auberge à Lapide* (Inv. no 83–3), a pen and pencil drawing taken from life that Ducros later made into a wash drawing for Ten Hove (vol I, fol 66/2); also the water-colour sketches of figures (Inv. D-83–1) that the painter used for several of the sketches in Amsterdam (vol III, fol 23/2 and fol 24/1).

54   Le site de la Maison d'Horace
The site of Horace's villa

Pen and black ink, water-colour, paper laid down on cardboard
$21\frac{1}{2} \times 29\frac{3}{4}$ in (54·8 × 75·5 cm)

52

53

54

Provenance: Bought by J.-I. Gerning when living in Naples (1794–99); Gerning Bequest to the Freies Deutsches Hochstift, Frankfurter Goethe-Museum, June 1934
Literature: Gerning, 1802, vol II, pp 107–108, Chessex, 1984 (2), p 74 and no 11
Related works: —Two drawings, one squared for transfer, J WHATMAN paper (55 × 76 cm), Lausanne (MCBA)
—Pen and black ink drawing, squared for transfer, tracing paper (74 × 112 cm), Lausanne (MCBA)
—Engraving after Ducros' water-colour, reproduced Gerning, 1802, vol III

Freies Deutsches Hochstift, Frankfurter Goethe-Museum (Inv. XIa-gr-11487)

The valley of Licenza, north-east of Tivoli, whose beauties were sung by Horace, was chosen by the poet as the site for his small villa, built by his patron Maecenas around 35 B.C. From the middle of the eighteenth century this spot in the Sabine Hills became a place of interest. In his *Dissertazioni sopra la Villa di Orazio Flacco* of 1767, Domenico De Sanctis wrote of archaeological discoveries that allowed the site of Horace's villa to be precisely located. From that time on the *locus classicus* became a favourite stopping-off point for those travellers on the Grand Tour who had an interest in archaeology and a feeling for unspoilt nature. Allan Ramsay was one of these, as can be seen from an unpublished study entitled *An Enquiry into the Situation and Circumstances of Horace's Sabine Villa*. The drawings he made between 1777 and 1784, and the accompanying ones by Jacob More, are some of the first modern depictions of this site.[1] There are also the recently rediscovered views by J P Hackert,[2] which were well known at the time owing to the engravings after them by the Swiss B A Dunker. Ducros frequently stayed at Tivoli between 1780 and 1793, and the Lausanne collection from his studio contains several drawings and water-colours of nearby Licenza and Vicovaro. Two drawings of the site of Horace's villa and, notably, a large squared tracing would seem to suggest that there exists a large picture of this subject which has yet to be located, of which this water-colour is a medium-sized reduction. The style of the figures on the right is reminiscent of the work of Ducros' assistant in Naples. This water-colour may be dated 1793 or 1794, the *terminus ante quem* being the date it was bought by Gerning, no later than 1800.
Reminiscent of Gessner's idylls, this landscape was bought by Johann-Isaac Gerning, the son of an entomologist and collector from Frankfurt, who made a career as a diplomat and writer. He lived in Naples between 1794 and 1799 and mentions Ducros' activities there for the first time in a letter published in *Der Neue Teutsche Merkur* in 1798; he speaks of him a second time in his work *Reise dürch Oesterreich und Italien* of 1802 (see cat no 82). Noting that Ducros had painted the area around Tivoli, particularly Horace's villa, Gerning took his inspiration from a water-colour he had recently acquired to make the engraving on the title page of the third part of his book, a passage of which is devoted to the site (p 178).

[1] James Holloway, 'Two Projects to illustrate Allan Ramsay's Treatise on Horace's Sabine Villa', *Master Drawings*, 14 (1976), pp 280–86.
[2] *Philipp Hackert, 'Zehn Aussichten von dem Landhause des Horaz', 1780.* Goethemuseum, Düsseldorf, 1983, (introduction by Wolfgang Kroenig).

55   Pie VI visitant les travaux d'assèchement des Marais Pontins
Pius VI visiting the drainage works at the Pontine Marshes

Oil on canvas
48 × 67 in (122 × 170 cm)
Signed and dated: *DuCros 1786*

Provenance: Commissioned by Pius VI(?), Sotheby's 26.2.1975 (38) 'The Property of a Gentleman'; acquired by the Museo di Roma, 1975 (see cat no 56).
Literature: Cecilia Pericoli Ridolfini, 'Pio VI alle Paludi Pontine, *Bollettino dei Musei Communali di Roma*, Anno XXII (1975), no 1–4, pp 26–32; Pierre Chessex, Review of the Gagneraux Exhibition, Roma-Dijon 1983, *Zeitschrift für schweizerische Archäologie und Kunstgeschichte*, 41 (1984), pp 139–140

Museo di Roma, Palazzo Braschi

The *Pianura Pontina* is a marshy region south of Rome running along the Via Appia near Terracina. Drainage had always been a problem in this area, with its threat of malaria, and cultivation was almost impossible. The Romans had tried to improve the land, and further attempts were made by various popes including Leo X and Sixtus V, but to little avail.
In 1777 Pius VI commissioned the Bolognese engineer Gaetano Rappini, who set to work on hydraulic drainage and made a canal running parallel to the Via Appia, the *Linea Pio*, which runs into the sea at Terracina. The pontiff attached great importance to this enterprise and went to the site of the works every Easter from 1780 to 1796. He would stay at Terracina rather than at his usual country residence, Castel Gandolfo, and during this period the town became a temporary capital full of foreigners, diplomats, courtiers, artists and adventurers. Ducros wrote to the Genevan naturalist Charles Bonnet on 7th July 1783: 'I had the honour of accompanying His Holiness to the Pontine Marshes to see a view of which he would like me to do a large painting'.[1] No document concerning a commission of this kind has been found in the Vatican archives, but several other sources exist for this trip with the Pope. There are drawings from life in the Lausanne museum (fig L), this large oil painting, and another version (99 × 137 cm) at Pavlovsk (fig M). According to information provided by Michael Liebmann (All-Union Art Research Institute, Moscow) this painting was one of three by Ducros from Prince Potemkin's collection which Catherine the Great bought in 1792 and the Emperor Paul I transferred to Gatchina in 1799. The two other pictures represent *The Grand Duke Paul visiting the Forum* and *The Grand Duke Paul and The Grand Duchess Maria at Tivoli* (cat no 56).
The first, dated 1782, was a commission from the Grand Duke while staying in Rome in February and March of that year, as is confirmed by a letter from Charles Bonnet to Ducros (26th March 1783) which refers to 'the masterpieces you are sending to the Grand Duke of Russia and which will enrich his study'.[2] We do not yet know whether *Pius VI visiting the Pontine Marshes* was one of these 'masterpieces' or whether it was painted later. The Pavlovsk version was made into an engraving by Raffaele Morghen and published

fig. L   Ducros, *Pie VI et sa suite*, Lausanne (MCBA).

fig. M   Ducros, *Pie VI aux Marais Pontins*, Pavlovsk, Leningrad.

55

fig. N
Morghen after Ducros,
Les Marais Pontins,
Istituto Nazionale per
la Grafica, Calcografia,
Rome.

in a large edition around 1784–85 (fig N). Again in connection with the improvement work on the Pontine Marshes, Ducros published an engraving (area within border: 31·5 × 51·2 cm) in 1784, with a dedication to Pius VI and signed L R Du Cros DDD.

The painting from the Museo di Roma depicts Pius VI arriving with his retinue near Terracina and being greeted by the townsfolk. It is easy to recognize the setting at the bottom of the Monte Circeo which dominates the marshes. In the distance is the straight line of the Linea Pio and Terracina harbour with its sailing boats is on the right. In contrast to the naturalism of the background is a somewhat theatrical foreground with a triumphal arch on the left and some ancient ruins on the right. The group of arcadian peasants in the centre suggests a homage to Poussin by an artist keen to create an historical painting rather than a mere piece of reportage. The Pavlovsk version, although similar in scale, is painted in a much more realistic and direct manner and differs greatly from the work of 1786. First, it is painted from the opposite direction, facing south-west from the heights bordering the Pianura Pontina near Sezze, towards Monte Circeo and Isola Ponziane visible in the distance, Terracina being

in the background on the left. Second, the emphasis is placed on the Pope and the engineer presenting him with a plan of the works, while the Museo di Roma version is centred on the devotion of the peasants. Finally, the approach is reportage without artifice or classical reference, as if taken from life—a far cry from the carefully stage-managed monumental composition of the painting of 1786.

There is one possible explanation for the difference between these two versions of *Pius VI visiting the Pontine Marshes*, the Pavlovsk one painted around 1783 (certainly before 1785) and the Rome one dated 1786. Between these years several major pictures of Pius VI were produced by artists close to Ducros. In 1784 Louis-Jean Desprez painted two monumental works depicting the splendour of the ruling pontiff,[3] while in 1785 Bénigne Gagneraux painted his *Meeting of Gustave III with Pope Pius VI in the Museo Pio-Clementino*.[4] The success of his two friends with these pictures may have encouraged Ducros to start work on a large historical painting, thus explaining the difference in the later version of *Pius VI visiting the Pontine Marshes*. This is mere supposition but we do know that Ducros did not continue in this vein, being less gifted in oil painting than water-colour, and better disposed to landscapes than large official commissions.[5]

1   BPU, Geneva, MS. Bonnet, 37.
2   BPU, Geneva, MS. Bonnet, 76.
3   Andrea Busiri Vici, 'A Papal Ceremony by Desprez', *Apollo* LXXXV, (1967), pp 366–70; Nils G Wollin, 1935.
4   *Bénigne Gagneraux, un pittore francese nella Roma di Pio VI*, Academia di Francia, Rome, 1983, no 26.
5   One exception is an unlocated picture depicting one of Murat's military exploits (see A Borzetti, 1901, p 55).

56   Le Grand-Duc Paul et la Grande-Duchesse Maria à Tivoli
The Grand Duke Paul and The Grand Duchess Maria at Tivoli

Oil on canvas
36¼ × 54¼ in (92 × 138 cm)

Provenance: Prince Gregory Alexandrovitch Potemkin, purchased by Catherine II in 1799, transferred to Gatchina by Emperor Paul I in 1799. Lost in the middle of the nineteeth century. Private collection, Moscow. Purchased by the Pavlovsk Palace Museum, 1974
Related Works:—*La Grotte de Neptune à Tyvoly* etching by Raffaele Morghen, (23·4 × 34·6 cm) (fig O)
—Various sketches of the site, Lausanne (MCBA)

Pavlovsk Palace Museum

'Neptune's Grotto, near Tivoli, affords a sight which is both unique and extremely picturesque. At the foot of the mountain on which the town is situated there is a cavern hollowed into the rock, its entrance covered by water; through the vaulted arch formed by this entrance can be seen a great torrent of water falling with a crash. Daylight filters in through an opening in the vault which is placed exactly above the cascade. It is impossible to describe adequately the beauty of this scene, when the early morning sun rises above the steep rocks surrounding the cavern. Its rays fall exactly on the tumbling water. In the background, now brightly lit, the water casts its silvery sprays upwards; at the

Les Marais Pontins

entrance the dark uneven rock face and the black vault are partly lit by the reddish reflection of the sun's rays.'[1]

Placed exactly below the Temple of the Sibyl and facing the Great Cascade, Neptune's Grotto is one of the picturesque attractions of the gardens of the Villa Gregoriana, greatly enjoyed by the tourists who visit Tivoli. Landscape artists have frequently painted this site, although they usually depict a more general view including the Temple of the Sibyl. Ducros takes a much closer viewpoint which allows him to concentrate solely on the beauties of nature, particularly waterfalls, vegetation, and rocks. It is worth noting that he painted a pendant to this picture, *La Grand-Duc Paul et sa suite au Forum* (Pavlovsk, fig P) in which he emphasized the archaeological setting.

Between 1782 and 1785 Ducros painted several 'conversation pieces' in oil.[2] This type of portrait, fashionable since Pompeo Batoni painted his materpieces, was taken up by many including Ducros' fellow countryman Jacques Sablet.[3] But Ducros did not persevere in this particular field, being more at ease with the large water-colour landscapes which were to become his speciality after 1785.

The Grand Duke Paul Romanov was the son of Catherine II and became Tsar Paul I in 1796. He visited western Europe with his young wife Maria Feodorovna in 1781–82.[4] Travelling under the name 'Comtes du Nord', they arrived in Rome on 5th February 1782, then went to Naples and were back in the Eternal City from 23rd February to 16th March 1782. It was doubtless during this second stay, when they were in touch with Angelica Kauffmann, J. P. Hackert,[5] and others, that they were painted by Ducros.

Le Grand Duc Paul au Forum is dated 1782 and there is every reason to believe that the Tivoli picture was painted at the same time. In a letter to Ducros dated 26th March 1783, the Genevan naturalist Charles Bonnet mentions 'the masterpieces you are sending to the Grand Duke of Russia which will enrich his cabinet'.[6]

56

fig. O
Morghen after Ducros, *La Grotte de Neptune à Tyvoly*, Castello Sforzesco, Civica Raccolta delle stampe Achille Bertarelli, Milan.

fig. P
Ducros, *Le Grand-Duc Paul et sa suite au Forum*, Pavlovsk, Leningrad.

[1] F J L Meyer, *Les tableaux d'Italie*, op cit, p 137.
[2] He even ventured into history painting with a picture for the 4th Earl of Bristol *Cicero discovering the tomb of Archimedes*, whereabouts unknown (see *Memorie per le Belle Arti*, Rome, 1785, pp LV–LVII).
[3] Nantes, Lausanne, Rome 1985.
[4] See Eckardt, 1979.
[5] W. Krönig, 'Philipp Hackert und Russland,' *Wallraf-Richartz-Jahrbuch*, XXVIII (1966), pp 309–320.
[6] BPU, MS, Bonnet, 76.

THE MUSEO PIO-CLEMENTINO

Between 1787 and 1792 Ducros and Volpato published a series of fourteen large views of the Museo Pio-Clementino, ten horizontal and four vertical. The same technique had been used by Volpato for the reproduction of famous works since the 1770s, as in his versions of the Raphael *stanze*, Carracci's painted gallery in the Farnese Palace, and of monuments in and around Rome. The technique was line-etching, where only the outlines of the architecture and objects were reproduced. The details of the statues, the shadows, marble, and colouring where then added in water-colour in the studio by Ducros and his assistants. This produced great differences in colouring from one series to another, depending upon the quality of execution. The series from the Pfaueninsel Palace in Berlin were painted by Ducros himself (his name appears with Volpato's on some of the mounts) but are too fragile to be included in this exhibition (figs 8, 9, 10). Ducros mentions this series only once in his correspondence, in 1791: 'May I have the pleasure of offering you, before you leave Naples, my best wishes . . . and two proofs of our engravings of the Vatican'.[2] At present the series at Pfaueninsel is the only complete one known to have been coloured by Ducros; two single prints are at the Nationale Forschungs- und Gedenkenstätten der klassischen deutschen Literatur in Weimar. A series of anonymous copperplates at the Calcografia Nazionale in Rome (Istituto Nazionale per la Grafica, Inv. 1615/1–14) must be the plates for the original set of the views of the Museo Pio-Clementino.

The set in Munich came to light in 1980 and examples are displayed here out of documentary interest. Probably a later edition than the original set coloured by Ducros, it differs in colouring, while statues and shadows are clearly more rudimentary in execution. Moreover, certain objects from the museum do not appear, which would suggest a later date. For instance, there is no large basin in front of the *Apollo* (cat no 60), while it can be seen on the copperplate of the corresponding print from Pfaueninsel (fig 8). Such considerations and the fact that Ducros left Rome in 1793, suggest that the Munich set was probably published, or at least coloured at Volpato's works after 1794 without any contribution from Ducros.

[1] These views were probably published separately. They were certainly not all made at the same time, as becomes clear from the museum's chronology in C. Pietrangeli 'I Musei Vatican al tempo di Pio VI', *Bollettino Musei e Gallerie Pontificie*, II,2 (1959–74), Vatican, 1978, particularly pp 20–30.
[2] Letter to François d'Ivernois, Rome, December 30th 1791 (BPU, Geneva, MS fr 1299).

57

57 Galleria delle Statue con Cleopatra

Hand-coloured outline etching on paper, grey passepartout
$20\frac{5}{8} \times 29\frac{1}{2}$ in (52·6 × 75 cm)

Provenance: c 1800 listed in an inventory of Munich library (the 14 views in the set are contained in a portfolio bearing the arms of the Biblioteca Regina Monacensis)
Literature: Carl-Christian Horvath, *Potsdam's Merkwürdigkeiten*, Potsdam, 1798, (Pfaueninsel, p 232); Michel Huber, *Manuel des curieux et des amateurs de l'art*, vol IV, Paris, 1800 (ad vocem Volpato); Emilio de Tipaldo, *Biografia degli italiani illustri del secolo XVIII*, vol 8 (ad vocem Volpato); C. A. Petrucci *Catalogo generale delle stampe tratte dei rami incisi posseduti dalla Calcografia Nazionale*, Rome, 1953, no 1615; 'Glyptothek München 1830–1980', *Jubiläumsausstellung zu Entstehung- und Baugeschichte*, Munich, 1980, pp 604–608
Related works: —Copperplate (area within platemark: 52·8 × 74·4 cm), Istituto Nazionale per la Grafica, Calcografia, Rome, Inv. 1615/3
—Hand-coloured outline etching, Pfaueninsel

58

Palace, West Berlin, Inv. Gk. I.42007
—Hand-coloured outline etching,
s'-Gravenhage, col. HHH

Bayerische Staatsbibliothek, Munich,
(Inv. Res. 2 Arch. 170 m, no 7)

The statue gallery was extended from 1776 to
1778 and a new setting for the *Arianna-
Cleopatra* was created. The putti supporting the
crest of Pius VI above this *trompe l'oeil* niche
were carved by Sibilla between 1778 and 1782.[1]
The room leading off on the left is the Sala degli
Animali (see cat no 58).
   Comparison between this print and the one
from Pfaueninsel (fig 9) reveals weakness both
in colouring and in attention to detail. For
example, the engraved lines of the garlands of
Pius VI's crest have been covered up with paint,
and a frame has inexplicably been added to the
sketchbook of the man drawing in the centre.

[1]   C. Pietrangeli, op cit, p 15 .

58   Sala degli Animali con Tevere

Hand-coloured outline etching on paper, grey
passepartout
$20\frac{1}{4} \times 29\frac{1}{4}$ in (51·5 × 74·2 cm)

Provenance and Literature: See cat no 57
Related works: —Copperplate (area within
border: 51·4 × 73·7 cm), Istituto Nazionale per
la Grafica, Calcografia, Rome, Inv. 1615/10
—Hand-coloured outline etching, Pfaueninsel
Palace, West Berlin, Inv. Gk. I.42009

Bayerische Staatsbibliothek, Munich,
(Inv. Res. 2 Arch. 170 m, no 3)

59   Cortile del Belvedere con Laocoonte

Hand-coloured outline etching on paper, grey
passepartout
$20\frac{1}{4} \times 28\frac{3}{8}$ in (51·3 × 72·2 cm)

Provenance and Literature: See cat no 57
Related works: —Copperplate (area within
border: 51·2 × 72 cm), Istituto Nazionale per la
Grafica, Calcografia, Rome, Inv. 1615/12
—Hand-coloured outline etching, Pfaueninsel
Palace, West Berlin, Inv. Gk. I.42004

Bayerische Staatsbibliothek, Munich,
(Inv. Res. 2 Arch. 170 m, no 5)

If this print is compared with the corresponding
one from Pfaueninsel or with the original plate,
a difference in the decoration of the museum
becomes apparent (see fig 10). Between 1772
and 1777 the Cortile Ottagono was made into
the entrance of the new Museo Pio-Clementino.
The *gabinetti* around the Cortile were intended
to provide suitable settings for famous
sculptures, namely the *Laocoon, Antinous,
Apollo* and *Venus Felix*. The Munich prints
show the Cortile at a later stage when passages
to the various *gabinetti* were cleared of objects
that had separated them from the central
Cortile.

60   Cortile del Belvedere con Apollo

Hand-coloured outline etching on paper, grey
passepartout
$20\frac{5}{8} \times 29\frac{1}{8}$ in (52·3 × 74 cm)

Provenance and Literature: See cat no 57
Exhibited: Glyptothek München, 1980, op cit,
no 304
Related works: —Copperplate (area within
border: 51·8 × 72·9 cm), Istituto Nazionale per
la Grafica, Calcografia, Rome, Inv. 1615/11
—Hand-coloured outline etching, Pfaueninsel
Palace, West Berlin, Inv. Gk. I.42010 (fig 8)
—Hand-coloured outline etching, Goethe-
Museum, Weimar, reproduced in Holtzhauer,
1969, p 297

Bayerische Staatsbibliothek, Munich,
(Inv. Res. 2 Arch. 170 m, no 6)

59

61

61 Gallerie delle Statue

Hand-coloured outline etching on paper, grey passepartout
$20\frac{1}{2} \times 29\frac{3}{8}$ in (52·2 × 74·5 cm)

Provenance and Literature: See cat no 57
Exhibited: Glyptothek München, 1980, op cit, no 302
Related works: —Copperplate (area within border: 51·7 × 73·7 cm), Istituto Nazionale per la Grafica, Calcografia, Rome, Inv. 1615/8
—Hand-coloured outline etching, Pfaueninsel Palace, West Berlin, Inv. Gk. I.42008

Bayerische Staatsbibliothek, Munich,
(Inv. Res. 2 Arch. 170 m, no 8)

This is a view of the long part of the statue gallery (seen from the opposite direction to cat no 57), looking towards the Sala dei Busti (see cat no 62), with pictorial decoration completed by Christoph Unterberger between 1777 and 1780.[1]

[1] Olivier Michel, 'Peintres autrichiens à Rome dans la 2e moitié du XVIIIe siècle: Christoph Unterberger', *Römische Historische Mitteilungen*, 14 (1972), pp 175–198.

62

62 Sala dei Busti

Hand-coloured outline etching on paper, grey passepartout
$20\frac{1}{2} \times 29\frac{3}{8}$ in (52·1 × 74·4 cm)

Provenance and Literature: See cat no 57
Exhibited: Glyptothek München, 1980, op cit, no 303
Related works: —Copperplate (area within border: 51·8 × 73·5 cm), Istituto Nazionale per la Grafica, Calcografia, Rome, Inv. 1615/2
—Hand-coloured outline etching, Pfaueninsel Palace, West Berlin, Inv. Gk. I.42011

Bayerische Staatsbibliothek, Munich,
Inv. Res. (2 Arch. 170 m, no 11)

For reasons of conservation and conditions of loan cat nos 57–59 exhibited at Kenwood, cat nos 60–62 at The Whitworth Art Gallery.

Ducros in British Collections

63 A View of the Harbour at Pozzuoli near Naples

Pencil and water-colour, laid down on canvas
$13\frac{7}{16} \times 18\frac{7}{8}$ in (34·2 × 47·6 cm)

Inscribed: *Ducros fecit Pouzol 1778 Figures sur le balcon un cheval blanc*
Provenance: Colnaghi's, from whom purchased and presented by the Friends of the Whitworth Art Gallery, 1957
Exhibited: Whitworth Art Gallery, Manchester, 1983, no 67
Literature: Luke Herrmann, *British Landscape Painting of the Eighteenth Century*, 1973, p 81; Chessex, 1982, p 61, n 84; Chessex, 1984(1), p 431.

The Whitworth Art Gallery, Manchester (D/4/1957)

This view of the harbour at Pozzuoli (situated to the west of Naples) is one of the earliest dated examples of Ducros' work; it is related in style, subject and size to a number of drawings in a collection of some three hundred sketches and water-colours by Ducros now in the Rijksprentenkabinet, Amsterdam. In April 1778, Ducros was engaged to accompany a group of Dutchmen as draughtsman on a journey to the Kingdom of the Two Sicilies and Malta, returning to Rome in August 1778 (see cat nos 51–53); the drawings now in Amsterdam are those made by Ducros in the course of the expedition. As Pierre Chessex has pointed out, they may be compared with drawings made in the same year by a number of French artists under the leadership of Dominique Vivant-Denon, later published in the Abbé de Saint-Non's *Voyage pittoresque ou description des royaumes de Naples et Sicile*, 1781–86, or with those made by J P Hackert and the amateur Charles Gore in 1777 when they accompanied Richard Payne Knight to Sicily. Ducros' views, however, were not engraved for publication and remained unknown until very recently.[1] They were grouped into albums by the artist's patron and leader of the expedition, Nicolas Ten Hove, and at some time before their acquistion in 1948 by the Rijksprentenkabinet about a dozen drawings were removed from the volumes. This sheet is perhaps one of those. Many of the sketches seem to have been drawn on the spot, and include a wide range of subject-matter—landscapes and seascapes, careful drawings of archaeological sites, sketches of country people, sailors and fishermen. This view of Pozzuoli has inscriptions which suggest that Ducros intended to develop the subject further, presumably as a finished water-colour.

[1]   J. W. Niemeijer, 'Het reisverhaal van W C Dierkens in het Rijksprentenkabinet', *Nederlands Kunsthistorisch Jaarboek*, 1981.

63

64 The Basilica of Maxentius

Pencil, pen and brown ink, water-colour and gum arabic; J HONIG & ZOONEN paper
$16\frac{15}{16} \times 25\frac{1}{2}$ in (43·1 × 64·8 cm)

Inscribed (verso): *Tempio della Pace*
Provenance: ?Henry Thomas, 2nd Earl of Ilchester (1747–1802); by descent; Sotheby's 14th June 1973 (lot 138, as Clérisseau); Agnew's; presented by the National Art-Collections Fund, 1973
Exhibited: City Art Gallery, Manchester, *Eighty Years On: Treasures from Galleries in the North West acquired with the help of the NA-CF 1903–1983*, 1983, no 11; Whitworth Art Gallery, Manchester, 1983, no 68
Literature: F J Mejanes, 'A Spontaneous Feeling for Nature', *Apollo*, CIV (1976), p 403.
Related works:—Three pen drawings, Lausanne (MCBA); pen drawing, preparatory to the etching, Lausanne (MCBA); etching with water-colour, by Ducros and Volpato; water-colour versions, differing slightly in viewpoint and staffage, are in the Yale Center for British Art, New Haven (signed and dated 1779) and Lausanne (MCBA), see cat no 5

The Whitworth Art Gallery, Manchester (D/12/1973)

Among the grandest of the ruins of Imperial Rome, these vaults were known until well into the nineteenth century as the Temple of Peace (as the inscription on the verso of this drawing indicates). In fact, the three enormous bays formed the north aisle of a vast basilica, begun by Maxentius during his brief reign, A.D. 306 to 312, and completed by Constantine. In this water-colour, Ducros shows the Colosseum on the right, but, unlike the other versions (see cat no 5) does not include the Campanile of S. Francesca Romana.

83

64

Pierre Chessex has suggested that this composition was one which Ducros may have made with the assistance of a camera obscura (see cat no 5). This may well be so, but Ducros' wide-angle, dramatic choice of viewpoint, emphasising the massive scale of the structure, must surely have been influenced by Piranesi's etching of the same subject from the same angle in his *Vedute di Roma*.

This water-colour is one of four by Ducros from the collection of the Earls of Ilchester whose house, Melbury, was not far from Stourhead.[1] It was perhaps Sir Richard Colt Hoare who was responsible for this commission from Ducros.

[1] These were sold at Sotheby's 14th June 1973, lots 137–140, attributed to C L Clérisseau: *The Colosseum, The Basilica of Constantine* (ie *The Basilica of Maxentius*), *The Church of S. Lorenzo in Miranda, The Arch of Vespasian* (ie *The Arch of Titus*).

65 The Interior of the Colosseum

Hand-coloured outline etching
20½ × 29 in (51·8 × 73·5 cm)

Inscribed: l'Interieur du Colisé and on wash border *78 Ducros et Volpato f* with Ducros' initials in monogram
Provenance: From the library of King George III which was presented to the British Museum by King George IV, 1823; transferred from the Map Room to the Department of Prints and Drawings, 1952
Related works:—Pen and pencil drawing, Lausanne (MCBA)
—Water-colour, commissioned by Richard Colt Hoare, Stourhead, see cat no 70
—Water-colour, Lausanne (MCBA), see cat no 4
—Several impressions of the etched outline, together with counter-proofs, all uncoloured, Lausanne (MCBA)
—Water-colour study for this coloured etching, signed and dated 1780, Lausanne [MCBA)

The Trustees of the British Museum
(1952-4-3-8)

Cat nos 65–67 are from the series of hand-coloured etchings published by Ducros and Volpato, *Vues de Rome et de ses environs*, the first twenty-four of which appeared in 1780. An account of the technique employed in producing these large prints will be found on p 20. As Pierre Chessex notes, their novelty and popularity lay in their impressive scale and in the fact that although they were prints, the skilful use of delicately etched lines, washes of water-colour and touches of gouache resulted in a quality which can make them pass for original water-coloured drawings. The origins of this technique can be found in the work of Ducros' fellow Swiss artist Johann Ludwig Aberli (1723–86), who had developed a method for duplicating Swiss views and rustic subjects, by which the outlines of popular compositions were engraved and then completed with water-colour or gouache—the 'manière Aberli', patented in Bern in 1766. Ducros' knowledge of these popular Swiss prints, together with Volpato's experience as a highly skilled reproductive engraver, combined to produce a handsome series of prints which appealed to contemporary taste, partly perhaps as updated and 'swagger' versions of a genre dominated since the late 1740s by Piranesi's views of the city. The Ducros/Volpato prints were at the same time close enough in compositon to several of Piranesi's most celebrated designs to satisfy conventional taste yet quite different in mood.

The Colosseum, in its picturesquely overgrown and ruinous state, was a popular sketching ground for artists from the sixteenth century until the late nineteenth century, when the luxuriant growth of plants and flowers which gave the ruin much of its romantic quality was finally cleared away. In 1744 Pope Benedict XIV consecrated the arena of the Colosseum to the memory of the Christians martyred there; a central cross and its stations were set up—several of which can be seen here and in other versions of this composition.

This composition—one which Ducros repeated on several occasions—was among those published in 1780. It would be interesting to know if the British artists, John 'Warwick' Smith and Francis Towne, who both made impressive water-colours of the interior of the Colosseum, knew Ducros' etching. Smith's large-scale views (in the British Museum) have a grandeur that exceeds anything painted by his contemporaries, and Ducros could perhaps have seen some of them, although it should be said that there is no evidence of this. The vast scale and magnificence of the Colosseum exerted a particular attraction on artists towards the end of the eighteenth century.

65

66 The Villa Montalto-Negroni

Hand-coloured outline etching
$20\frac{1}{4} \times 29$ in ($51\cdot2 \times 73\cdot6$ cm)

Inscribed: La villa Negroni and on wash border
66 Ducros et Volpato with Ducros' initials in
monogram
Provenance: See no 65
Related works:—Water-colour, Lausanne
(MCBA), see cat no 12

The Trustees of the British Museum
(1952-4-3-9)

This is from the series of seven views of gardens
of the most celebrated villas in Rome, etched
and published by Ducros and Volpato c.1782–
84. They are among the most decorative
examples of such large-scale prints, this view in
particular echoing something of the mood of
Hubert Robert's drawings and etchings of
Italian scenes. This coloured etching is very
similar in composition to the original water-
colour (cat no 12), although there are minor
differences in the number and grouping of the
figures.
　The Villa Montalto-Negroni (so-called after
the family of the original owner, Cardinal
Montalto, who became Pope Sixtus V, and also
after the most important subsequent owners, the
Negroni family) was sold in 1784 to a
speculator, who dispersed the contents of the
villa and sold off parts of the garden. The most
notable item in the collection was Bernini's
marble group of *Neptune and Triton*, which had
stood in the gardens and was subsequently
acquired by Sir Joshua Reynolds (now in the
Victoria and Albert Museum).

67 The Baths of Caracalla

Hand-coloured outline etching
$20 \times 29\frac{1}{4}$ in ($50\cdot7 \times 73\cdot9$ cm)

*Inscribed: Du Cros e Volpato f Vue de Termes
de Caracalla* and on wash border *41 Ducros et
Volpato f* with Ducros' initials in monogram
Provenance: See cat no 65
Related works:—Water-colour of the
Tepidarium of the Baths of Caracalla, Lausanne
(MCBA), see cat no 10
—Two water-colours of the Baths of Caracalla,
Musée de Berne

The Trustees of the British Museum
(1952-4-3-10)

The site of the Baths of Caracalla was of
particular interest to Ducros' partner, Giovanni
Volpato, who, like several other artists of the
period (notably Gavin Hamilton) also acted as
an archaeologist and was granted permission by
Pope Pius VI in 1779 to excavate among the
ruins. It was not however until the next century
that systematic excavations began and the
vegetation was cleared: indeed, it was the
romantic neglect of the site that had attracted
artists to sketch its crumbling grandeur. The
poet Shelley was later to describe 'the flowery
glades and thickets of odoriferous blossoming
trees which extend in ever-winding labyrinths
upon its immense platforms and dizzy arches
suspended in the air' (Preface to *Prometheus*,
1819).

66

68 View at Tivoli

Water-colour and gouache on paper laid down
on canvas
26×40 in ($66 \times 101\cdot5$ cm)

*Inscribed (*on the canvas backing*): Grotte de
Neptune pour monsieur le chevalier Hoare de cher
Du Cros*
Provenance: Sir Richard Colt Hoare, 2nd Bart.
(1758–1838); by descent
Literature: Richard Colt Hoare, *The History of
Modern Wiltshire*, vol I, 1822, p 83; Kenneth
Woodbridge, *Landscape and Antiquity: Aspects
of English Culture at Stourhead 1718 to 1838*,
1970, p 96 and pl 31b

The National Trust, Stourhead
(Hoare Collection)

In February 1787 Richard Colt Hoare wrote to
his half-brother Hugh, 'Du Cros an artist . . .
whom I think I mentioned to you last year has
done four drawings for me which (if they arrive
safe in England) will be the admiration of the
whole town & put all our English artists . . . to
the blush'.[1] This view of the Falls of Tivoli was

67

68

among the first group of works by Ducros acquired by Colt Hoare; he was subsequently to commission a further seven water-colours and two hand-coloured outline etchings, all of which are still at Stourhead and comprise the most complete collection of the artist's work to be seen in England.

Colt Hoare—like many other visitors to Rome—found Tivoli even more beautiful than he had anticipated. 'I never mean to quit this place, indeed it has temptations enough to seduce any man who has a proper taste for the beauties of Nature. This small spot . . . contains more picturesque scenes & a greater variety of objects than any place I have ever seen'.[2] With his passion for classical history and literature, the associations of Tivoli were irresistible and he could not but 'feel a degree of enthusiasm, on breathing the same air as Brutus, Cassius, Sallust, Horace, Propertius'.[3]

Of the first group of four water-colours by Ducros bought by Colt Hoare, this is certainly the most dramatic in design, and in handling. The composition is indebted to Vernet (whose paintings had been particularly popular with British patrons), but in execution is a striking example of Ducros' virtuoso handling of water-colour, particularly in the depiction of the cascading water. As the Swiss critic Bridel later noted, 'Ducros observed that we never see objects through a pure medium, but through an atmosphere which, vaporous to a greater or lesser extent, always modifies colours'.[4] As a visitor to Stourhead in the 1790s, the young Turner would surely have been impressed by such examples of Ducros' water-colours as this, with its combination of the Sublime and the Picturesque.

[1] Richard Colt Hoare to Henry Hoare, 21 February 1787.
[2] Richard Colt Hoare to Henry Hoare, 29 April 1786.
[3] Richard Colt Hoare, *Recollections*, I, 1817, p 97. All three quotations are taken from Woodbridge, 1970, *passim*.
[4] Bridel, 1803

69 Beneath the Villa of Maecenas, Tivoli

Water-colour and gouache with varnish on several pieces of paper, laid down on canvas
$29\frac{1}{2} \times 42\frac{1}{2}$ in (75×108 cm)

Inscribed (on the canvas backing): *L'intérieur des Ecuries de Mecenas*
Provenance: See cat no 68
Literature: Colt Hoare, 1822, p 83; Woodbridge, 1971, p 97
Exhibited: *Souvenirs of the Grand Tour*, Wildenstein, London, 1982, no 22
Related works:—Two pen drawings on tracing paper, Lausanne (MCBA)
—Water-colour (a reduced version of this composition), Lausanne (MCBA); see cat no 21

The National Trust, Stourhead
(Hoare Collection)

One of the most dramatic of all Ducros' compositions, this 'souterrain view', as Colt Hoare described it, shows the ruins of the Santuario di Ercole Vincitore, long thought to be the remains of the Villa of Maecenas at Tivoli: in the late eighteenth century this area beneath the Villa was thought to have been—as the inscription on the canvas backing shows— the ancient stables. No impression of an etching of this composition is known, although Ducros included a view of the Villa in the catalogue of the stock sold by his print shop. Cat no 21 is a later, smaller version of this water-colour, probably based on a tracing, a practice habitually followed by Ducros as a simple method of reproducing his compositions. This water-colour is one of the second group acquired by Colt Hoare after 1786.

Both in general conception and in handling of chiaroscuro, Ducros' water-colour clearly owes a debt to Piranesi's engraved views of the Villa of Maecenas, the interior of Hadrian's Villa and the series, *Dell'Emissario del Lago Albano*. To some extent, this could also be regarded as an example of *paysage historique*—an imaginary reconstruction of a period in antiquity, set in a landscape. Ducros could have been influenced by the works of Jakob Philipp Hackert in his introduction of vaguely appropriate classical figures: in most of Ducros' Roman views, he made a point of introducing contemporary onlookers.

70 The Interior of the Colosseum

Pencil, water-colour, gouache with touches of pen and ink and varnish on two sheets of paper laid down on canvas
30×44 in (76×112 cm)

Inscribed (on the canvas backing): *Vue de l'interieur de Colise*

69

Provenance: See cat no 68
Literature: Colt Hoare, 1822, p 83
Related works:—Water-colour, Lausanne
(MCBA); see cat no 4
—Pen and pencil drawing, Lausanne (MCBA)
—Several impressions of the etched outline,
together with counter-proofs, all uncoloured,
Lausanne (MCBA)
—Hand-coloured outline etching from the
Ducros and Volpato studio, 1780; see cat no 65
—Water-colour study for the coloured etching,
signed and dated 1780, Lausanne (MCBA)

The National Trust, Stourhead
(Hoare Collection)

Ducros made a number of views of the
Colosseum, depicting on different occasions
both the exterior and the interior. The earliest
example included in this exhibition is a coloured
etching, published by Ducros and Volpato in
1780, cat no 65. This water-colour, painted for
Colt Hoare circa 1786, shows the interior from
a slightly different angle, and is more broadly
handled, while the figures are grouped in a more
sophisticated and dramatic manner. In the left
foreground, two elegantly dressed women are
shown giving alms to a begging family, while
their male companion admires the Colosseum;
in the background a crowd of people are taking
part in a religious ceremony.
Cat no 4 is a later version of the same
composition, probably copied from this water-
colour in all essentials, though the figures were
redrawn later, partly to allow for a change of
style in dress.

71 The Arch of Constantine

Water-colour and gouache on several pieces of
paper laid down on canvas
$30\frac{3}{4} \times 43\frac{3}{16}$ in ($78\cdot1 \times 109\cdot8$ cm)

Inscribed: (on the canvas backing): *L'arc de
Constantin*
Provenance: See no 68
Literature: Colt Hoare, 1822, p 83
Exhibited: Souvenirs of the Grand Tour,
Wildenstein, London, 1982, no 22
Related works:—A very similar version, later in
date, Lausanne (MCBA), see cat no 2; etched
outline, in reverse, Lausanne (MCBA)

The National Trust, Stourhead
(Hoare Collection)

The arch was erected in honour of Constantine,
to commemorate his victory over Maxentius in
A.D. 312, and was completed three years later:
the sculpture and reliefs decorating the arch
were chiefly taken from earlier monuments. As
can be seen both from this water-colour and cat
no 2 (which is probably slightly later in date),
the base of the arch was still partly buried in the
late eighteenth century. It was not until 1804-05
that Pius VII had the arch excavated down to
the ancient pavement (see cat no 6).
Colt Hoare described this water-colour (which
is from the second group he commissioned from
Ducros, circa 1788–93) as 'one of the most
laborious as well as one of the most happy
efforts that were ever made in water-colour'.

72 The Falls of the Velino into the River Nera

Water-colour and gouache over pencil
$30\frac{3}{4} \times 63$ in ($76\cdot8 \times 157\cdot5$ cm)

70

Provenance: See cat no 70
Literature: Colt Hoare 1822, p 83;
Woodbridge 1970, pp 80–82, 96
Exhibited: Souvenirs of the Grand Tour,
Wildenstein, London, 1982, no 26
Related works:—Pen and pencil drawing,
Lausanne (MCBA)
—Water-colour with pen and black ink,
heightened with gouache and oil, Lausanne
(MCBA), see cat no 25
Both of these depict the 'Cascata di Terni in
primo piano'.
—Versions of the present composition are at
Lausanne (MCBA) and Dunham Massey.

The National Trust, Stourhead
(Hoare Collection)

Ducros' large-scale water-colours of the
waterfalls at Terni and at Tivoli were among the
most popular subjects with his British patrons.
This composition was among the first of
Ducros' large water-colour designs, in which he
began to specialize circa 1784. Ducros is
recorded as having painted views of the Falls of
Terni and the Falls of Tivoli for Lord
Breadalbane circa 1784–85 (the whereabouts of
both are unknown), and another of the Cascade
at Terni (also untraced) for John Campbell,
later 1st Lord Cawdor, who visited Italy in 1784

71

and again in 1786–88; his collection of twelve water-colours by Ducros was sold at Christie's 6th June 1800, when a view of the Temple at Tivoli fetched 101 guineas (noted by the diarist Joseph Farington as a remarkable large sum, and considerably more expensive than a Cuyp sunset landscape in the same sale, which realized only 84 guineas),[1] that of the Cascade at Terni selling for 32 guineas. Later versions of this composition include one painted for Lord Grey in 1787 or 1788, now at Dunham Massey (the artist's receipt of 18th April 1788 for £25 survives), and the version exhibited here, which was among the second group of water-colours commissioned from Ducros after 1786 by Richard Colt Hoare.

Ducros' mastery in depicting waterfalls was noted by contemporary critics, an article in the *Memorie per le Belle Arti* for April 1785 especially praising the two water-colours painted for Lord Breadalbane: 'As the water cascades precipitously from on high, it disperses into an immense quantity of the tiniest drops, which spread like a white mist, veiling surrounding objects and blurring them, making the colours and outlines unclear. This observation, neglected by many, has not escaped Monsieur Ducros who has imitated to perfection the moist and misty air, and has rendered with the very greatest success the haziness with which we see everything enveloped in such vapours . . . these two pictures are very precious because the most beautiful and elusive accidents of Nature are there faithfully transcribed and painted with grace and harmony'.[2]

Colt Hoare was immensely impressed with the grandeur of the cascade, finding it, as the novelist Smollett had in 1764, 'an object of tremendous sublimity'. He noted that 'it is reckon'd the highest in Europe, and the water is a very white hue which Virgil mentions'.[3] His last visit to Terni was in October 1789, when he walked along the banks of the Nera: 'At one time buried in the deep recesses of a high-grown forest . . . emerging from this dark retreat, the long expected object of attention burst upon my sight, and left no further scope for imagination; for the fall of the Velino into the Nera is one of those wonderful works of nature, which no mind can fancy, nor pencil delineate with appropriate grandeur'.[4] Ducros' rendering of the subject was subsequently, however, to be praised by Colt Hoare: 'One of the great excellences of the Artist was the just and natural delineation of water, particularly where spray and vapour were expressed; and in this subject [i.e. *The Falls of the Velino*] he has succeeded most admirably, and without any of the borrowed assistance of white paint'.[5]

In composition, this water-colour is very similar to that painted for Lord Grey, although the Dunham Massey version perhaps places more emphasis on the cascade of water by including less foreground detail on the left. The figures are quite different in each version, presumably painted by Ducros' assistant on his instructions. By contrast with cat no 25, the present composition is less monumental in effect, chiefly because of the horizontal format.

1   A copy of the catalogue of Lord Cawdor's collection, sold at Christie's, 5–6th June 1800, in the Department of Prints and Drawings, British Museum, is marked with the prices fetched by the twelve Ducros water-colours, together with others by Tito Lusieri and Henry Tresham. See also Francis Russell, 'A Distinguished Generation: the Cawdor Collection', *Country Life*, 14th June 1984, pp 1746–48.
2   *Memorie per le Belle Arti*, Rome, 1785, pp LV–LVII.
3   Richard Colt Hoare, MS Journal, Wiltshire Archaeological Society, Devizes, p 77.
4   Richard Colt Hoare, *Recollections Abroad*, 1815–18, vol II, p 252.
5   Richard Colt Hoare, *The History of Modern Wiltshire*, 1822, vol I, p 83.

73

73　The Arch of Titus

Probably hand-coloured outline etching
28¾ × 20 in (73 × 58 cm)

Provenance : See cat no 68
Related works :—Water-colour, Lausanne
(MCBA), see cat no 1
—Water-colour, commissioned by 2nd Earl of
Ilchester, Fondation Custodia, Paris

The National Trust, Stourhead
(Hoare Collection)

As well as eight large water-colours
commissioned by Colt Hoare, he also owned
two examples of Ducros' popular views of
Roman antiquities which are probably hand-
coloured etchings—*The Forum of Nerva with the
Colonacce* and *The Arch of Titus.* An etching of
this size was included in the catalogue of
coloured prints sold by Ducros (see Appendix
2). The composition of this version is exactly
similar, though considerably reduced in size, to
a water-colour in the studio collection at
Lausanne (cat no 1). On this occasion, Ducros
seems to have retained the large original water-
colour, and sold only smaller versions (one of
these belonged to Colt Hoare's neighbour, Lord
Ilchester). The dress and the slightly stiff
handling of the figures compares with other
coloured etchings of the early 1780s—see cat
nos 65–67.
Ducros' compositional source here is surely
Piranesi; but the Arch of Titus was depicted by
countless artists of the period.

74　The Temple of Minerva Medica

Pencil, water-colour and gouache on paper, laid
down on canvas
26½ × 40½ in (67·3 × 102·9 cm)

Provenance : Probably commissioned from the
artist by George, Lord Grey, later 6th Earl of
Stamford (1765–1845); by descent
Literature : St J Gore, 'Portraits and the Grand
Tour', *Apollo,* CVIII (1978) pp 24–31, fig 2;
Chessex, 1982, p 62 and fig b
Related work :—water-colour and gouache
(67·3 × 103 cm), Dunham Massey
—Pen and ink drawing (66.5 × 102 cm)
Lausanne (MCBA)
—Outline etching by Ducros and Volpato
(50.3 × 73.7 cm)

The National Trust, Dunham Massey
(Stamford Collection)

Two views of the Temple of Minerva Medica
which cost £50 for the pair, including 'Glaces et
Bordures', and the Cascate delle Marmore at
Terni at £25, are noted in a receipted bill
submitted by Ducros to Lord Grey, paid on
18th April 1788. Lord Grey, later 6th Earl of
Stamford (1765–1845), had a tutor in Rome in
1786 who was a Swiss compatriot of Ducros,
Auguste Pidou. That Pidou knew Ducros is
evident from his journal, in which he recorded
visiting the artist's studio in 1784 at the time
that Ducros was working on a painting
commissioned by Lord Bristol, *Cicero
discovering the Tomb of Archimedes.*[1]
The so-called Temple of Minerva Medica (in
fact a Nymphaeum, or perhaps a hall for
ceremonial gatherings) was probably the central
section of extensive thermae built in the Licinian
Gardens for the Emperor Gallienus (A.D. 235–
268). By the late eighteenth century it had
become one of Rome's most frequently depicted
ruins. Ducros' two water-colours show the
structure from slightly different viewpoints; in
the water-colour at Dunham Massey (fig Q) it
appears to be at some distance from the
spectator, an effect enhanced by showing the
party of visiting tourists, who have come to
admire the Temple, on a diminutive scale. In the
present view the ruin is seen from close to, and
more attention is concentrated on the figures, a
group of peasants who are using the Temple and
its immediate surroundings to grow
vegetables—a contrast between the glory of
Rome's past and impoverished, albeit
picturesque, state of affairs at the end of the
eighteenth century. The overgrown appearance
of the ruin can be seen in other paintings and
drawings (for instance, Richard Wilson's
painting of circa 1753–54, in the collection of
Brinsley Ford), but Ducros has
characteristically exaggerated the effect. The
colouring of this pair of water-colours—cold,
steely tones of grey, blue and dark green, with
stormy skies—is impressive and anticipates the
dramatic atmospheric qualities of his late works.

[1]　Louis Vulliemin, *Un magistrat suisse : Auguste Pidou,
Landammann du Canton du Vaud. Notice historique,*
Lausanne, 1860, p 27.

74

fig. Q   Ducros, *Temple of Minerva Medica*, National Trust, Dunham Massey.

75

75   The Temple of the Sibyl, Tivoli

Water-colour, on a page in a sketchbook used by John Flaxman in Italy, chiefly when in Rome circa 1787–94
Sketchbook $5\frac{3}{4} \times 7\frac{1}{2}$ in (15.6 × 19 cm)

Inscribed (below the water-colour, in Flaxman's hand) : *Temple of the Sybil at Tivoli—Du Cros*
Provenance : Bought at Christie's 1865; by descent
Literature : David Irwin, *John Flaxman 1755–1826*, 1979, p 53
Related works : Among Ducros' numerous views of the Temple of the Sibyl, the following are most closely related :
—Water-colour, formerly in the collection of the Earls of Harrowby, Sandon Hall, now in Birmingham Museum and Art Gallery
—Uncoloured etching, Geneva (BPU)

Private Collection

As Flaxman noted in a letter to his parents in January 1790, 'I have no reason to be discontented with Rome, for I have been treated with particular attention by most of the artists of the first eminence, both Englishmen and foreigners'.[1] The present sketchbook seems partly to have been used by Flaxman as an album to which various friends contributed, including the French architect Charles Percier and Ducros. This water-colour is the only evidence that the two men knew one another. It must predate Ducros' departure from Rome in February 1793.
In its simple, unaffected style, this study recalls the sketches made by Ducros in 1778 during his tour of Southern Italy and Sicily (see cat nos 51–53). It has every appearance of being drawn on the spot and since Tivoli was, according to the artist's own correspondence, one of his favourite places, it is tempting to think that it might have been made on a sketching trip (perhaps even in company with Flaxman).
Other variants of this view by Ducros are in a more familiar and elaborate style, notably the water-colour now in Birmingham, which has the usual overabundance of foliage and is more consciously 'atmospheric'.

[1]   Flaxman to his parents, 26th January 1790. British Library, Add. MS. 39780 f. 47 v.

76   The Greek Theatre at Syracuse

Water-colour
$11\frac{1}{2} \times 15\frac{1}{4}$ in (29·2 × 38·7 cm)

Trustees of the Victoria & Albert Museum (P.4-1950)

In July 1789 Ducros was described by Bridel as 'at present working on a Sicilian project, containing twenty-four views of that famous island'. However, this series of prints, which was to have been published in collaboration with Pier Paolo Montagni, never seems to have been engraved, despite a prospectus issued by Ducros in 1799. The artist's letter of December 1800 to Richard Colt Hoare (Appendix 1) mentions the fact that he proposed a series of views of Sicily and Malta, which, however, had not yet been engraved.[1]
Ducros had first visited Sicily in 1778 (see cat nos 51–53), but he seems to have gone there again in the winter of 1788–89 in connection

with this project. Very few drawings of Sicilian subjects from the latter part of Ducros' career are known; the largest group of studies, together with some etchings and tracings are in Lausanne. Only three landscapes, besides this view of the theatre at Syracuse and the spectacular *Storm at night, Cefalù* (cat no 41) have so far been traced.

This water-colour shares much of the same dramatic quality as no 41. The sweeping composition,[2] in which the curve of the theatre and the distant hills and silhouette of the town seem to act as a frame for the sky, is among Ducros' most Sublime designs.

[1]   See 'Historical and Biographical Notes', p 24.
[2]   It is perhaps not too fanciful to discern a similar compositional formula to that used by J R Cozens in the late 1770s and 1780s, which Ducros may have known.

77   Launching a ship, Castellammare

Water-colour with gouache and varnish on several pieces of paper, laid down on canvas
$27\frac{1}{2} \times 41\frac{3}{4}$ in (70 × 106 cm)

Provenance: Painted for Sir John Acton, 6th Bart. (1736–1811); thence by descent
Related works:—See cat no 38

Private Collection

Together with cat nos 78 and 79, this is one of a group of six water-colours painted by Ducros for Sir John Acton, circa 1794–96.[1] Born in Franche-Comté (where his father had settled), Acton had entered the naval service of Tuscany, where his talents had been recognized by the Grand Duke Leopold, brother of Queen Maria Carolina of Naples. In 1779, he was appointed to undertake the reorganization of the Neapolitan navy, at a critical period in the country's history. Within a short time, the direction both of the foreign policy of the Kingdom and of internal administration was in his hands. He was appointed Minister of War and the Marine, and later of finance, and ultimately his paramount influence was formally acknowledged when he was appointed Prime Minister. The aim of the Queen of Naples was to play a prominent part in the politics of Europe—an aim which made the reorganization of the navy and army a prime necessity. When Acton entered the service of Naples, the fleet was almost non-existent. Under him, the shipbuilding yard at Castellammare was modernized, skilled engineers and technicians were brought from abroad, and the revival of sea trade encouraged. Six new ships of the line were launched from Castellammare within six years, and by 1798 the fleet comprised about one hundred and fifty ships large and small. This intensive activity is commemorated in four large water-colours painted by Ducros which show various aspects of the shipyards. Of all Ducros' works, these—not surprisingly—most clearly reflect the influence of Vernet's marine paintings, notably the series depicting the *Ports of France*. Acton may originally have owned a larger series: Johann Isaac Gerning[2] recorded that he had 'a room full of varnished gouaches' by Ducros. The present work, the launching of the *Tancred* (rather than that now in Lausanne, cat no 38), seems to fit Gerning's description of one of the series: 'particularly superb . . . is the launching of a warship against a background of

76

the chestnut-covered slopes of Castellammare, in the presence of the royal family and a large crowd'.

[1]   Acton's Neapolitan career is described in Harold Acton, *The Bourbons of Naples 1734–1825*, 1956.
[2]   J I Gerning, 1802 (see Bibliography).

78   Interior of a fort at Naples

Water-colour with gouache and varnish, laid down on canvas
$28\frac{3}{8} \times 41\frac{3}{8}$ in (72 × 105 cm)

Provenance: See cat no 77

Private Collection

No contemporary description of this water-colour appears to have survived, and it is hoped that the opportunity of including it in the exhibition will lead to a fuller identification of the event depicted.

As General of the Neapolitan army and Minister of War, Acton reorganized military affairs in the Kingdom. The infantry were trained in the Austrian style, the artillery modelled on the French and the cavalry on the Prussians. Officers were sent to France and Austria to study army administration and the most up to date engineering inventions. Acton

77

78

also improved the defences of Naples, and planned new roads to improve communications in the country. He established an important new armaments factory and ironworks at Torre Annunziata, while the arsenal was said to be one of the best in Italy.

It has been suggested that this water-colour may show the interior of the Castel dell'Ovo in Naples. Ducros' painting seems to commemorate a royal visit to a military establishment: the central figures are, to judge from documented portraits, King Ferdinand IV and Queen Maria Carolina. The figure on the left, in military uniform, could perhaps be General Acton.

79   The Chinese Pavilion

Water-colour with gouache and varnish
$25\frac{5}{8} \times 37\frac{3}{8}$ in (65 × 95 cm)

Inscribed: Pavilon Chinois dans la Forêt près du Cazin de son Excellence S.E. Monsieur le General Acton à Castelmara 1794
Provenance: See cat no 77

Private Collection

The variety and range of Ducros' style can be seen by comparing this charming, decorative work with his views of the naval dockyards at

79

Castellammare which are in the same collection. This water-colour appears to be unique in Ducros' *œuvre*, and was presumably a special commission from Acton. As a record of a neo-classical garden, somewhat in the English taste, with wooded walks on a hillside, it is of considerable interest. Queen Maria Carolina had a *jardin anglais* at Caserta, which could have inspired a local fashion among members of the Court circle. The pavilion ('chinese' only in the most whimsical sense) gives the composition the air of a stage set for an opera.

The elegant figures, as in other works of Ducros' Neapolitan period, are probably by the unidentified 'Venetian assistant' noted by J-I Gerning (see 'Historical and Biographical Notes', p 23).

80   Letter from Ducros to Sir Richard Colt Hoare

National Trust, Stourhead (Deposited in the Wiltshire Record Office)
See Appendix 1

This is the only surviving letter from Ducros to his patron Sir Richard Colt Hoare, written from Malta on 22nd December 1800. As Ducros told Colt Hoare, 'I have been taken to Malta now to paint views for General Graham who has conquered this place'. Thomas Graham, later Lord Lynedoch (1748–1843) had been in command of the British blockade of Malta, which had been occupied by the French: Bonaparte's troops surrendered in September, Ducros arrived from Messina, where he had met Graham, in November and stayed until May 1801. Five views of Valletta by Ducros are now in the island's Museum of Fine Arts, numerous drawings are in Lausanne, and a water-colour panorama of Malta is on loan to the Château de Wildegg, Switzerland.

Ducros' letter describes the beauty of the island—'en un mot je retrouve Claude Laurin et Vernet à chaque instant'. But the real purpose of the letter was an attempt to secure Colt Hoare's patronage and the attention of his friends, as well as of booksellers and print dealers, for the scheme to engrave a series of twenty-four views of Sicily and Malta to be sold by subscription. Ducros hoped to appeal to Colt Hoare's patriotic feelings—'c'est un sujet national . . . Malthe Minorque et Giberaltar sont les boulevards de la Puissance Britanique'. In the event, only one etching of Malta was made (see cat no 49). In the same letter, Ducros also noted that Lord Elgin was said to have been pleased with two large drawings he had had sent to him in Constantinople, and that he had expressed a wish to commission from Ducros a series of views of monuments of ancient Rome, like those he had commissioned from Tito Lusieri (a well-known topographical artist of the period).

81   Richard Colt Hoare
'The History of Modern Wiltshire' 1822, Vol. I

The British Library Board

The first volume of *The History of Modern Wiltshire*, intended by Colt Hoare as a sequel to *The Ancient History of Wiltshire*, 1812–21, to which he had been the chief contributor and moving spirit, was published in 1822. It dealt with *The Hundred of Mere*, in which Stourhead was situated, and recorded the history of the area from the Domesday Book to modern times. It was in his description of the house that he included the passage concerning his collection of Ducros' water-colours and an assessment of his influence on the British school of water-colourists (see cat nos 68–73 and the essay 'Ducros and the British').

82 Johann-Isaac Gerning
'Reise dürch Oesterreich und Italien', 1802, Vol. III

Stadt u-Universität Bibliothek, Bern

Johann-Isaac Gerning, a German diplomat, lived in Naples between 1794 and 1799, when he came to know Ducros. In a letter published in *Der Neue Teutsche Merkur*, 1798, Gerning noted that Ducros' water-colours 'are sold at very high prices in England by his protector Hamilton'. Ducros had first met Sir William Hamilton in 1778, and later received a commission from him:[1] as Minister Plenipotentiary to the Court at Naples, Hamilton was influential both among Italians and English visitors, and Ducros doubtless cultivated this aquaintance. It was perhaps through Hamilton that Ducros met Sir John Acton (see cat nos 77–79), whose collection of water-colours by the artist was noted by Gerning in his *Reise dürch Oesterreich und Italien*.
Gerning devoted part of Vol. III of *Reise . . .* to a description of the supposed site of Horace's Sabine villa, noting that Ducros had often painted in the area, and illustrating the book with an engraved frontispiece after a water-colour by Ducros in his possession (see cat no 54).

[1]   A drawing in pen and pencil of *The Arch of Titus* (related to cat nos 1 and 73), Lausanne, MCBA, is inscribed with a note in Hamilton's hand which records a commission of 18th March 1791 for several water-colours from Ducros: 'Je sousigné déclare avoir donné ma commission a Monsr Ducros à Rome le 18 Mars 1791 de différents dessins qui sont chez moi à Naples et de lui avoir payé cette grandeur suivant ses prix d'alors à Trente livres Sterling. Wm Hamilton'.

Hoc erat in votis

82

BIBLIOGRAPHY

1779
Fuesslin, Johan Caspar, *Geschichte der besten Künstler in der Schweiz*, Vol 5, Zurich, 1779 (ad vocem La Croix).

1781
Meusel, Johann Georg (ed.), *Miscellaneen artistischen Inhalts*, Book 9, Erfurt, 1781.

1783
'Quelques petites choses sur les Beaux-Arts', *Etrennes Helvétiennes curieuses et utiles pour l'An de Grace 1783*, Lausanne.

1784
'Diario Ordinario', no 972, 24th April 1784, *Roma nella Stamperia Cracas*.

1785
Memorie per le Belle Arti, Rome, I, 1785.

1786
Meusel, Johann Georg (ed.), *Miscellaneen artistischen Inhalts*, Book 28. Erfurt, 1786.

1787
Huber, Michel, *Notice générale des graveurs . . .*, Dresden and Leipzig, 1787.
Hirt, Aloïs: see 1979 Eckardt.
Meusel, Johann Georg (ed.), *Museum für Künstler und Kunstliebhaber*, Mannheim, 1787.

1789
R B, 'Lettre adressée aux Rédacteurs', *Journal de Genève*, no 41, 17th October 1789.
An amateur, 'Lettre adressée aux Rédacteurs', *Journal de Genève*, no 43, 31st October, 1789.

1790
(Bridel, Jean-Louis-Philippe), 'Lettre sur les artistes suisses maintenant à Rome' (28th July 1789), *Etrennes Helvétiennes et patriotiques pour l'An de Grace 1790*, no VIII, Lausanne.

1796
(Hennezel, Béat de), 'Lettre au rédacteur du Journal Littéraire de Lausanne', *Journal littéraire de Lausanne*, VI, 1796.
Piranesi, Francesco, *Lettre de François Piranesi à Monsieur le général D. Jean Acton . . .*, Stockholm, n.d. (1796).

1797
Meusel, Johann Georg (ed.), *Neue Miscellaneen artistischen Inhalts*, Leipzig, 1797.
Huber, Michel and Rost C C H, *Manuel de curieux et des amateurs de l'art . . .*, Vol 1, London, 1797.

1798
Gerning, Johann Isaac, 'Kunstnachrichten, Neapel, bis zum 30 April 1798', *Der Neue Teutsche Merkur*, October 1798, Vol 3, part 10.

1800
Huber, Michel, *Manuel des curieux et des amateurs de l'art . . .*, vol IV, Paris, 1800.

1802
Gerning, Johann Isaac, *Reise dürch Oesterreich und Italien*, Frankfurt am Main, 1802, 3 vol.
Bruun Neergaard, 'De l'etat actuel des arts à Genève', Tonnes Christian, Paris, An X.
Fernow, Karl Ludwig, *Sitten und Kulturgemälde von Rom*, Gotha, 1802.

1803
(Bridel, Jean-Louis-Philippe), 'Lettre sur quelques artistes suisses', (Rome, 1st May 1802), *Etrennes Helvétiennes et patriotiques pour l'An de Grace 1803*, Lausanne.

1805
Schlegel: see 1846.
Goethe: see J. H. Meyer, Leipzig, 1969.
(Wagner, Sigmund), 'Etwas über dem Maler Sablet von Morsee genant der Römer . . .', *Journal für Literatur und Kunst*, Book 3, Zurich, 1805.

1806
Fuessli, Johann Rudolph, *Allgemeine Künstlerlexikon*, Zurich, II, 1806.

1807
Guattani, Giuseppe Antonio (ed.), *Memorie enciclopediche romane sulle Belle Arti . . .*, Rome, vol II (1807?).

1808
Notizie degli intagliatori raccolte da vari scrittori ed aggiunte a Giovanni Gori Gandellini dal Padre Maestro Luigi de Angelis, vol. IV, Siena, 1808, chap. XXII.

1809
Fernow, Karl Ludwig, 'Bericht aus Rom November 1808', *Journal des Luxus und der Moden*, January, 1809.
Wagner, Sigmund, see *Neujahrsblatt . . .*, 1889.
Histoire du Pays de Vaud par un Suisse, Lausanne, 1809.

1810
Koenig, Franz Niklaus, *Description de la Ville de Berne . . .*, Bern, 1810.
Wagner, Sigmund, 'Kunstausstellung', *Neues Allerley über Kunst, Kunst-Sinn, Geschmack, Industrie und Sitten*, Part 14, Bern, 1810.

1811
Notizie degli intagliatori . . ., vol IX, Siena, 1811 (ad vocem Ducros and Montagnani).

1812
Lutz, Markus, *Nekrolog denkwürdiger Schweizer . . .*, Aarau, 1812 (ad vocem Ducros).

1816
Notizie degli intagliatori . . ., vol XV, Siena, 1816 (ad vocem Volpato).

1817
Dellient, François, *Tableau historique du Canton*

de Vaud en Suisse, Manuscript, vol 1, BCU, Lausanne, 1817–18.

1821
(Chavannes, Daniel-Alexandre), 'Instruction Publique, Musée Cantonal', *Feuille du Canton de Vaud*, vol 8, 1821.

1822
Colt Hoare, Sir Richard, *The History of Modern Wiltshire*, vol I, London, 1822.

1824
Journal d'Alméras: see Dolt, 1938.
Palmerini, Niccolo, *Opere d'intaglio del cav R. Morghen*, Florence, 1824.

1832
De la Rive, Pierre-Louis, *Notice biographique de M. P.-L. De la Rive, peintre de paysage, membre de la Société des Arts*, Geneva, 1832.

1834
Tipaldo, Emilio de, *Biografia degli italiani illustri del secolo XVIII*, 10 volumes, 1834–45 (vol 8, ad vocem Volpato).
Chavannes, Daniel-Alexandre, 'Le Musée Cantonal. Ducroz. Kayserman. Mullener et Brandoin', *Journal de la Société vaudoise d'utilité publique*, XXI, 1835.

1841
Chavannes, Daniel-Alexandre, 'Notice historique sur le Musée Cantonal', *Journal de la Société vaudoise d'utilité publique*, XXVII, 1841.
Catalogue des plâtres, tableaux à l'huile, aquarelles et gravures exposés dans les salles du Musée Arlaud le 1er janvier 1841, époque de son ouverture au public, manuscript, MCBA Lausanne.
'Le Musée Cantonal et le Musée Arlaud', *Revue Suisse*, IV, 1841.

1846
(Lardy, Charles), *Catalogue des objets d'art exposés dans le Musée Arlaud*, Lausanne, 1846.
Schlegel, August Wilhelm, 'Schreiben an Goethe über einige Arbeiten in Rom lebender Künstler im Sommer 1805', *Sämtliche Werke*, IX, Leipzig, 1846–47.
Bryan, Michael, *Biographical and Critical Dictionary of Painters and Engravers*, London, 1849.

1859
(Birmann, Joanna), 'Der Landschaftmaler Peter Birmann von Basel', *Neujahrsblatt der Künstlergesellschaft in Zurich für 1859*, XIX.

1860
Vulliemin, Louis, *Un magistrat suisse. Auguste Pidou, Landammann du Canton de Vaud. Notice historique*, Lausanne, 1860.

1861
Tischbein: see 1922.

1868
Dubois-Melly, Charles, *P-L de La Rive et les premières expositions de peinture à Genève, 1796–1834*, Geneva, 1868.

1870
Archinard, Charles, *Histoire de l'instruction publique dans le Canton de Vaud*, Lausanne, 1870.

1876
Rigaud, Jean-Jacques, *Renseignements sur les Beaux-Arts à Genève*, Geneva, 1876.
Catalogue des tableaux du Musée Arlaud, Lausanne, (1876).

1889
Baudot, Henri, *Eloge historique de Bénigne Gagneraux*, 2nd edition, Dijon, 1889.
(Wagner, Sigmund), 'Aus dem Briefwechsel des Berner Kunstfreundes Sig. Wagner mit David Hess, I', *Neujahrsblatt der Künstlergesellschaft in Zurich für 1889*.

1900
Borzelli, Angelo, 'L'Academia del disegno a Napoli nella seconda metà del secolo XVIII', *Napoli Nobilissima*, IX–X, 1900–01.

1903
Baud-Bovy, Daniel, *Peintres genevois, 1702–1817*, I, Geneva, 1903.

1905
Bonjour, Emile, *Le Musée Arlaud (1841–1904)*, Lausanne, 1905.
Brun, Carl, *Schweizerisches Künstler-Lexikon*, Frauenfeld, I, 1905.

1906
Montaiglon, Anatole de and Guiffrey, Jean-Jules (ed), *Correspondance des Directeurs de l'Académie de France à Rome . . .*, 18 vols, Paris, 1887–1912, cf XV (1906), XVII (1908).

1910
Guiffrey, J and Marcel, P, *Inventaire général des dessins du Musée du Louvre, Ecole française*, V, Paris, 1910.

1911
Severy, M. and Mme William de, *La Vie de Société dans le Pays de Vaud à la fin du XVIIIe siècle*, Paris and Lausanne, vol II, 1911.

1912
Hautecoeur, Louis, *Rome et la renaissance de l'antiquité à la fin du XVIIIe siècle*, Paris, 1912.

1914
Gilliard, Charles, 'Un voyage en Italie à la fin du XVIIIe siècle', *Bibliothèque Universelle et Revue Suisse*, Jan/Feb, 1914.
Thieme, Ulrich and Becker, Felix (ed.), *Allgemeines Lexikon der bildenden Künstler von der Antike bis zur Gegenwart*, X, Leipzig, 1914.

1922
Tischbein, Wilhelm, *Aus meinem Leben*, Berlin, 1922.

1927
Agassiz, Daisy, *A. L. Du Cros, peintre et graveur, 1748–1810*, Lausanne, 1927 (printed separately from *Revue Historique Vaudoise*, 1927).

1928
Agassiz, Daisy, 'Un paesagista svizzero a Roma: Luigi Rodolfo Du Cros', *Roma, rivista di studi e di vita romana*, VI, 1928, pp 545–552.
Whitley, William Thomas, *Artists and their Friends in England, 1700–99*, vol II, London, 1928.

1929
Agassiz, Daisy, *Les frères Sablet*, Lausanne, 1929 (printed separately from RHV, 1929).

1930
Bonello, Vincenzo, 'Maltese water-colours by A Du Cros and D. Roberts', *Bulletin of the Museum, Malta*, I, 1930, pp 95–100.
Agassiz, Daisy, *François Keiserman. Un paysagiste suisse à Rome, 1765–1833*, Lausanne, 1930 (printed separately from RHV, 1930).

1933
Wollin, Nils Gustav, *Gravures originales de Desprez ou exécutées d'après ses dessins*, Malmö, 1933.

1935
Bell, C F and Girtin, T, 'The Drawings and Sketches of John Robert Cozens', *The Walpole Society*, XXIII, 1934–35.

1938
Salvagnini, Francesco, *I pittori Borgognoni Cortese e la loro casa in Piazza di Spagna*, Rome, 1938.
Dolt, Gustave, *Journal d'un artiste à Paris écrit par Maurice A Alméras (1824)*, Geneva, 1938.
Reau, Louis, *L'Europe française au siècle des lumières*, Paris, 1938.

1939
Bertarelli, Achille and Arrigoni, Paola, *Piante e vedute di Roma e del Lazio conservate nella raccolta delle stampe e di disegni*, Castello Sforzesco, Milan, 1939.

1943
Hugelshofer, W., *Schweizer Kleinmeister*, Zurich, 1943.

1944
Binyon, Robert Laurence, *English Water-Colours*, London, 2nd edition, 1944.

1946
'Valletta and the Grand Harbour in Nelson's days and now', *The Illustrated London News*, 4th May 1946, pp 496–97.

1948
Bovy, Adrien, *La peinture suisse de 1600 à 1900*, Basle, 1948.

1950
Zeltner Edmond and Schnegg, Alfred, 'Une vue du Locle (vers 1800)', *Musée Neuchâtelois*, 37, 1950, pp 3–7.

1951
Constable, W G, 'Carlo Bonavia and some Painters of vedute in Naples', *Beiträge f. Georg Swarzenski*, Berlin, 1951, pp 198–204.

1952
Oppé, A. Paul, *Alexander and John Robert Cozens*, London, 1952.

1953
Manganel, Ernest, 'Musée Cantonal des Beaux-Arts Lausanne, artistes vaudois du XVIIIe siècle à aujourd'hui', *Le Canton de Vaud, 1803–1953*, Lausanne, 1953.
Petrucci, Carlo Alberto, *Catalogo generale delle stampe tratte dai rami incisi posseduti dalla Calcografia Nazionale*, Rome, 1953.

1955
Lemaître, Henri, *Le paysage anglais à l'aquarelle, 1760–1851*, Paris, 1955.

1956
Verdone, Mario, 'Carriera romana dell' aquarellista Du Cros', *Strenna dei romanisti*, Rome, 1956, pp 206–212
Logoz, Roger-Charles, 'Un tableau de Ducros dans l'ancienne collection royale de Caserta', *Gazette de Lausanne, supplément littéraire*, 1st–2nd September 1956, p 7.

1958
Weinbrenner, Friedrich, *Denkwürdigkeiten*, Karlsruhe, 1958.

1961
Führer durch das Frankfurter Goethemuseum, Frankfurt am Main, 1961

1967
Honour, Hugh, 'Statuettes after the Antique. Volpato's Roman Porcelain Factory', *Apollo*, LXXXV (1967), pp 371–3.

1968
Herrmann, Luke, 'The William Spooner Collection and Bequest', *The Burlington Magazine*, CX (1968), p 401.
Apollonj Ghetti, Fabrizio M., *L'Arcipelago Pontino nella storia del medio Tirreno*, Rome, 1968.

1969
Meyer, Johann Heinrich, introduction to Goethe J. W., *Winckelmann und sein Jahrhundert in Briefen und Aufsätzen*, Leipzig, 1969 (first published Tübingen, 1805).
Gore, St John, 'Pictures in National Trust Houses', *The Burlington Magazine*, CXI (1969), April supplement.
Boyer, Ferdinand, *Le monde des arts en Italie*, Turin, 1969, pp 157–63.
Holtzhauer, Helmut, *Goethe-Museum*, Berlin and Weimar, (1969).
Faccioli, C, 'Anni ed epistolario romani d'un grande incisore Bassanese, G Volpato, 1733–1803', *L'Urbe*, 32, 1969, pp 18–35.

1970
Belloni, C, 'I pittori delle paludi pontine e del Circeo', *L'Urbe*, 3, 1970.
Woodbridge, Kenneth, *Landscape and Antiquity: Aspects of English Culture at Stourhead 1718 to 1838*, Oxford, 1970.

1971
Pietrangeli, Carlo, *Il Museo di Roma. Documenti e iconografia*, Bologna, 1971.
Berger, René, *Promenade au Musée des Beaux-Arts de Lausanne*, Lausanne, 1971.
De Rossi, Giovanni Maria, *Torri costiere del Lazio*, Roma, 1971.
Reynolds, Graham, *A Concise History of Water-colours*, New York, 1971.
Woodbridge, Kenneth, *Stourhead, Wiltshire*, The National Trust, 1971.

1972
Morsier, Georges de (ed.), 'Lettres du peintre P.-L. De la Rive pendant son séjour en Italie (1784–86)', *Geneva*, 20, 1972, pp 231–318.
Kroenig, Wolfgang, 'Storia di una veduta di Roma', *Bollettino d'Arte*, 57, 1972, pp 165–198.

1973

Herrmann, Luke, *British Landscape Painting of the Eighteenth Century*, London, 1973.

1974

Ford, Brinsley, 'William Constable, an Enlightened Yorkshire Patron', *Apollo*, XCIX (1974), pp 408–415.

Ford, Brinsley, 'James Byres, Principal Antiquarian for the English Visitors to Rome', *Apollo*, XCIX (1974), pp 446–461.

Gage, John, 'Turner and Stourhead: the Making of a Classicist?', *The Art Quarterly*, XXXVII (1974), pp 59–87.

Causa Picone, Marina, *I disegni della Società Napoletana di Storia Patria*, Naples, 1974.

Sutton, Denys, 'Magick Land', *Apollo*, XCIX (1974), pp 392–407.

1975

Deuchler, F, Luethy, H, and Roëthlisberger, M, *La peinture suisse du Moyen Age à l'aube du XXe siècle*, Geneva, 1975.

Pericoli Ridolfini, C, 'Pio VI alle Palude Pontine', *Bollettino dei Musei Communali di Roma*, 1975, pp 26–32.

Hardie, Martin, *Water-colour Painting in Britain*, 3 vol, London, 3rd edition, 1975–79.

1976

Castelnuovo, Enrico, 'Ducros, maître réputé du paysage pittoresque ou sublime', *Encyclopédie illustrée du Pays de Vaud*, VI, Lausanne, 1976, pp 112–115.

Mejanes, J F, 'A spontaneous feeling for Nature: French 18th Century Landscape Drawings', *Apollo*, CIV (1976), pp 396–404.

Zeri, Federico, 'La percezione visiva dell'Italia e degli italiani nella storia della pittura' *Storia d'Italia*, VI, Turin, 1976.

1977

Bacou, Roseline, *French Landscape Drawings and Sketches of the 18th Century*, The British Museum, 1977.

Briganti, Giuliano, *I pittori dell'imaginario. Arte e rivoluzione psicologica*, Milan, 1977.

1978

Gore, St John, 'Portraits and the Grand Tour', *Apollo*, CVIII (1978), pp 24–31.

Hardtwig, Barbara, *Bayerische Staatsgemäldesammlungen, Neue Pinakothek, München, Band 3: Nach-Barock und Klassizismus*, Munich, 1978, no 12526.

1979

Van de Sandt, Udolpho, 'L'art français de la fin du 18e siècle à Rome: index des artistes français . . .', *Bulletin de la Société de l'histoire de l'art français(1977)*, Paris, 1979, pp 171–178.

Irwin, David, *John Flaxman, 1755–1826. Sculptor, illustrator, designer*, London, 1979.

Eckardt, Götz (ed.), *Ein Potsdamer Maler in Rom. Briefe des Batoni-Schülers J. G. Puhlmann aus den Jahren 1774 bis 1787*, Berlin (DDR), 1979.

Wilton, Andrew, *The Life and Work of J. M. W. Turner*, London, 1979.

1980

Wilton, Andrew, *Turner and the Sublime*, London, The British Museum, 1980.

Wodon, Bernard, 'Nicolas de Fassin, portraitiste de Voltaire', *Livres et Lumières au pays de Liège*, Liège, 1980.

Van de Sandt, Udolpho, 'La chalcographie des frères Piranesi: quelques avatars de la gravure au trait', *Bulletin de la Société de l'histoire de l'art français*, 1978, Paris, 1980, pp 207–220.

1981

Sandstroem, Birgitta, *Bénigne Gagneraux 1756–1795. Education, inspiration, oeuvre*, Stockholm, 1981 (Dissertation, University of Stockholm).

Clark, Anthony Morris, 'Roma mi è sempre in pensiero', *Studies in Roman 18th Century Painting*, Washington, 1981, pp 125–138.

Grandjean, Marcel, 'Aperçu sur l'histoire de l'Art à Lausanne'. *Les monuments d'Art et d'Histoire du Canton de Vaud*, IV, Lausanne and Basle, 1981.

Lees-Milne, James, *Coughton Court, Warwickshire*, The National Trust, 1981.

Niemeijer, J W 'Het reisverhaal van W C Dierkens in het Rijksprentenkabinet', *Nederlands Kunsthistorische Jaarbook*, XXXII (1981).

1982

Hawes, Louis, *Presences of Nature. British Landscape 1780–1830*, New Haven, Yale Center for British Art, 1982.

Bjurstroem, Per, *French Drawings. Eighteenth Century*, Nationalmuseum, Stockholm, 1982 (Drawings in Swedish Public Collections no 4).

Chessex, Pierre, 'Quelques documents sur un aquarelliste et marchand vaudois à Rome à la fin du 18e siècle: A L R Ducros (1748–1810)', *Revue Historique Vaudoise*, XC (1982), pp 35–71.

1983

Tittoni Monti, Elisa, 'Volpato e Roma', *Piranesi e la Cultura Antiquaria, Attic del Convegno* 1979, Rome, 1983.

Hugli, Jean, 'Histoire et préhistoire d'une école d'art', *Cette Ecole d'Art*, Lausanne, Iderive, 1983, pp 7–113.

Koschatzky, Walter, *Die Kunst des Aquarells. Technik, Geschichte, Meisterwerke*, Salzburg and Vienna 1983 (2nd edition).

Wilton, A and Joll, E, *J M W Turner*, Paris, Grand Palais, 1983, nos 83 and 84.

1984

Van de Sandt, Anne, *Jacques Sablet (1749–1803). Biographie et catalogue raisonné*, Paris, 1984 (Dissertation, Université Paris IV).

Russell, Francis, 'A Distinguished Generation. The Cawdor Collection', *Country Life*, 14th June 1984, pp 1746–1748.

Chessex, Pierre (1), 'A Swiss Painter in Rome: A L R Ducros', *Apollo*, CXIX (1984), pp 430–37.

Chessex, Pierre (2), 'Ducros 'italienische Landschaften. Die Landschafts-wahrnehmung eines Schweizer Malers am Ende des 18. Jahrhunderts', *Daidalos, Berlin Architectural Journal*, 12th June 1984, pp 70–78.

Niemeijer, J W 'Een Grand Tour in beeld. Viet Hagenaars in 1778 met een Zwitserse vedutentekenaar op reis door Italië', *Herinneringen aan Italie*, 's-Gravenhage, Rijksdienst Beeldende Kunst, 1984, pp 63–67.

PREVIOUS EXHIBITIONS

1789

Geneva, Salon de la Société des Arts. *Notice des tableaux et des portraits exposés dans le Sallon de la Société des Arts*, nos 27, 29 and 37.

1792

Geneva, Salon de la Société des Arts. *Notice des tableaux, miniatures et dessins fait par des Genevois, exposés au Sallon de l'Académie*, nos 11, 12, 18 and 19.

1810

Bern, Schweizerische Kunst-und Industrieaustellung. (No catalogue, see Wagner, 1810)

1933

Lausanne, Exposition d'aquarelle de Ducros sous les auspices de la Société Vaudoise des Beaux-Arts. No catalogue.

1953

Lausanne, Musée Cantonal des Beaux-Arts. *Aquarelles de Abraham-Louis-Rodolphe Ducros, 1748–1810*, Introduction by Louis Junod.

1954

Rome, Istituto Svizzero. *Acquerelli di A L R Ducros, pittore svizzero, 1748–1810*. Preface by Luc Boissonnas.

1955

Rome, Palazzo Braschi. *Mostra di vedute romane appartenenti alla raccolta del Barone Basile de Lemmerman*, pp 29, 30, 39, 42, 43. Catalogue by G Incisa della Rocchetta.

1957

Naples, Palazzo Reale. *Vedute napoletane della raccolta Lemmerman*, no 54. Catalogue by Gino Doria.

1959

Rome, Palazzo delle Esposizioni. *Il settecento a Roma*, nos 196, 1230, 1344, 1409.

1961

Rome, Palazzo Braschi. *I Francesi a Roma*, no 783

1961

Paris, Hôtel de Rohan. *Les Français à Rome*, no 726

1961

Versailles, Château de Versailles *Malte, huit siècles d'histoire*, nos 257, 258.

1962

Naples, Palazzo Reale. *Il paesaggio napoletano*

nella pittura straniera, nos 30–33. Catalogue by R Causa (some exhibits not in catalogue).

1968

Bregenz, Vorarlberg Landesmuseum and Vienna, Oesterreichisches Museum für Angewandte Kunst. *Angelika Kauffmann und ihre Zeitgenossen*, fig 220.

1971

Rome, Farnesina. *Vedute romane: Disegni dal XVI al XVIII secolo*. no 102 (anonymous).

1974

Lausanne, Musée Historique de l'Ancien-Evêché. *Autour du Groupe de Coppet*, no 145.

1976

Lausanne, Musée Historique de l'Ancien-Evêché. *Gibbon à Lausanne*, nos 52–53.

1980

Lausanne, Musée Historique de l'Ancien Evêché. *Benjamin Constant (1767–1830) et Lausanne*, nos 157, 187, pl p 73.

1980

Rome, 5°Salone nazionale dell'antiquariato, Roma-EUR. *Roma e Tivoli nelle vedute dell'Ottocento*, p 84.

1981

New Haven, Yale Center for British Art. *Classic Ground: British Artists and the Landscape of Italy, 1740–1830*, no 62, catalogue by Duncan Bull.

1982

Stockholm, Nationalmuseum. *På Klassisk Mark. Målare i Rom på 1780-talet*, nos 71–74, 140–142, 173A–176.

1982

London, Wildenstein. *Souvenirs of the Grand Tour*, nos 22–27, catalogue edited by Denys Sutton.

1983

Manchester, The Whitworth Art Gallery. *The Draughtsman's Art. Master Drawings in the Whitworth Art Gallery*, nos 67 and 68.

1985

Nantes, Musées départementaux de Loire-Atlantique
Lausanne, Musée Cantonal des Beaux-Arts
Rome, Museo di Roma, Palazzo Braschi.
Les frères Sablet (1775–1815). Peintures, dessins, gravures, nos 76–87, text and notes by Anne Van de Sandt.

APPENDIX 1

**Letter from Ducros to Sir Richard Colt Hoare,
22nd December, 1800** (National Trust,
Stourhead, deposited in the Wiltshire Record
Office)

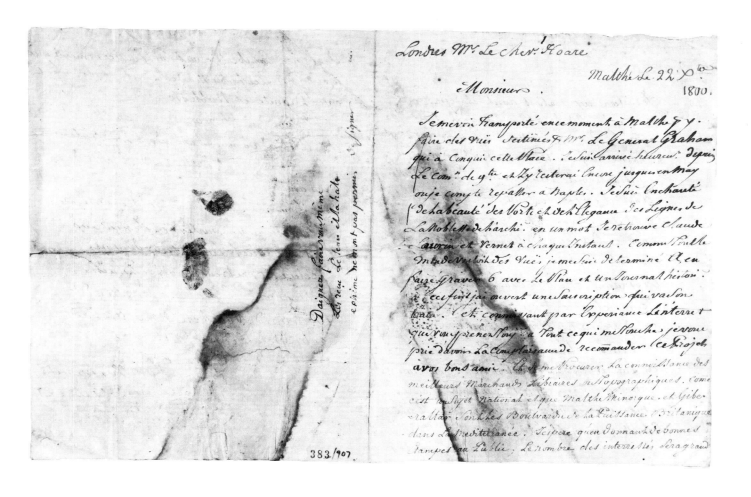

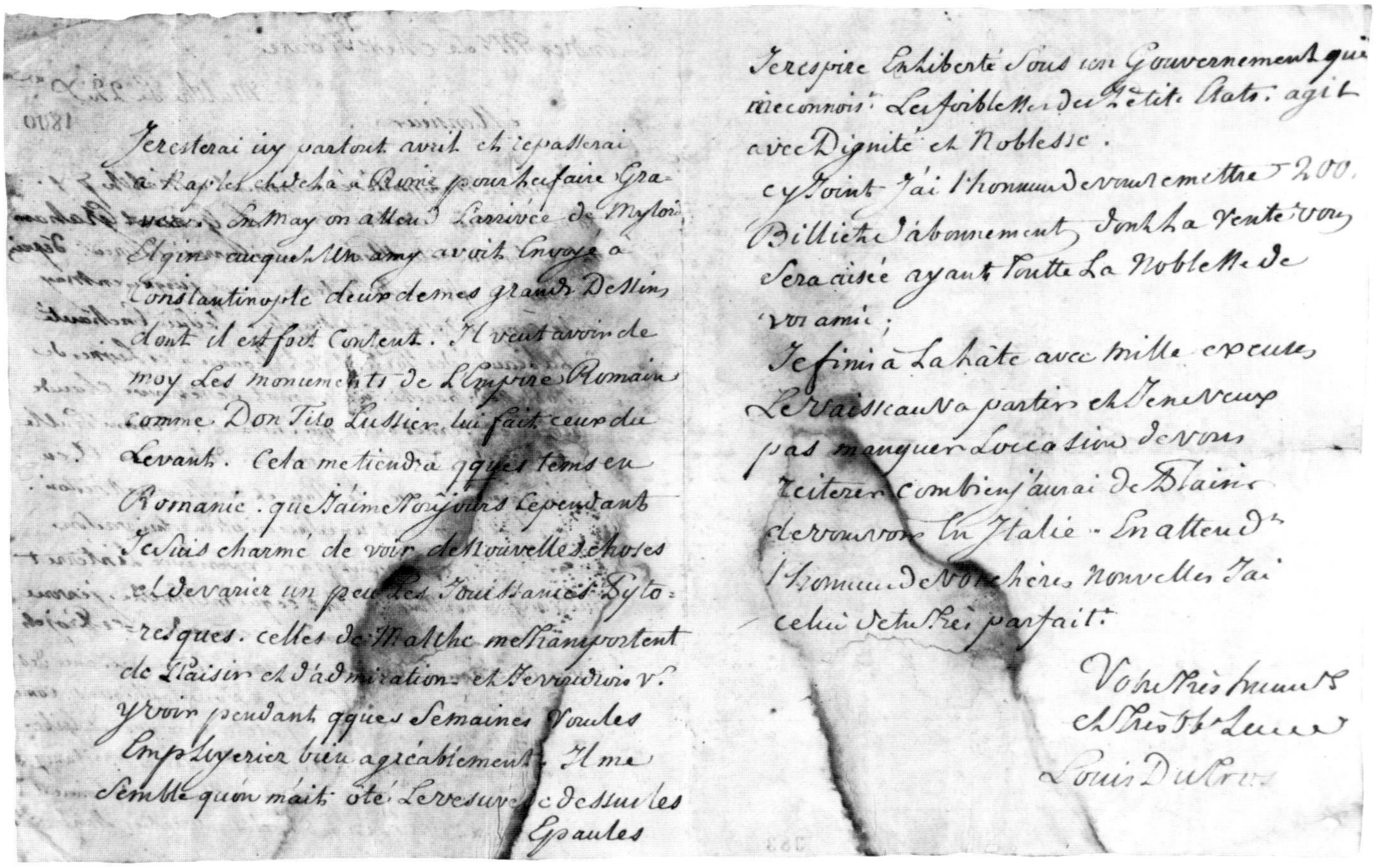

Je resterai icy partout avril et je passerai
à Naples et[c]h et à Rome pour y refaire Gra
ver. En May on attend l'arrivée de Mylord
Elgin auquel un amy avoit Envoyé à
Constantinople deux de mes grands Desseins
dont il est fort Content. Il veut avoir de
moy les monuments de L'Empire Romain
comme Don Tito Lusier lui fait ceux du
Levant. Cela me tiendra qques tems en
Romanie, que j'aime toujours. Cependant
Je suis charmé de voir de nouvelles choses
et de varier un peu les Jouissances Pyto-
resques. celles de Malthe m'ont transportent
de Plaisir et d'admiration. et je voudrois v.
y voir pendant qques Semaines. Vous les
Emp. y Vierier bien agréablement. Il me
Semble qu'on m'ait ôté Le resux e dessus les
Epaules

Je respire En Liberté Sous un Gouvernement qui
reconnoit Les foibleNes des P'tits Etats, agit
avec Dignité et Noblesse.
Cy Joint J'ai l'honneur de vous remettre 5 200.
Billiets d'abonnement, dont la Vente vous
Sera aisée ayant Toutte La NobleNe de
vos amis ;
Je finis à La hâte avec mille excuses
Le Vaisseau va partir et Je ne veux
pas manquer L'occasion de vous
reiterer Combiens j'aurai de Plaisir
de vous voir En Italie. En attend.
l'honneur de Vos chères Nouvelles J'ai
celui d'être parfait.

Votre Très humble
S. Très hble Lette
Louis DuCros

Letter from Ducros to the Directory,
1st April 1799, with a sale catalogue of the
Vues de Rome **and the** *Vues de la Sicile*
(Ministry of Foreign Affairs, Paris, Diplomatic
Archive, Corr. étr., Rome, vol 928, fol 261–262).

Gustave trois Roy de Suède qui se trouvoit alo
à Rome ait pu Empêcher L'Execution d'une Se
=tence dictée par la fausseté de ceux qui vouloi
m'éloigner pour s'élever sur les débris de mon Eta
=sement, Et occuper ma Place. Etabli depuis 25
dans cette Citté come artiste Suisse, J'avois fo
des commissions très considerables de Tableau
une collection de vües coloriées dont Je Joins
le Catalogue qui étoit, pour ma maison d'un gr
raport c'étoit comme une branche de Commerc
que J'avois ajouté a mes autres affaires qui au
à une Infinité de Jeunes Gens arrive En atte
=dant L'Epoque ou ils pussent aller par eux m
=mes. Le Gouvernement non content de m'avoi
Exilé et Ruiné, à Vermis le Pilliage de ma
maison, Et depuis cette Epoque n'a cessé de m
persécuter ici à Naples durant cinq ans, J
=ques au moment ou l'Armée d'Italie est
entrée à Rome.

Je viens d'aprendre Seulement dans le mois dernier à la
Suitte d'une course que J'ai faitte pour revoir Rome que
plusieurs personnes qui avoient Souffert Sous l'ancien
Gouvernement avoient étés dédomagés par un acte de
Justice de la Grande Nation. Ainsi Je Supplie le
Directoire envoyant combien J'ai Souffert d'ordoner
aux chefs de l'armée à Rome qu'ils aient à me faire
rembourser de 20 mille Livres par an Jusques à la
Somme totale de Cent mille Livres. Comme l'argent
y est rare, Je me cont'uterai de quelques bons table.
=aux d'Eglise ou de qques Statuës Il y en à tant
qu'une Copie peut remplacer pour l'Usage des croy=
=ans. Le cardinal Zelada fut inexorable et
Sa reponse fut. L'ordine Santissimo, conviene
obedire Subito. Le Directoire peut être plus
positif et plus Laconique En rendant Justice
à un artiste Vexé cruellement
un Seul acte de Sa Volonté Suffit.

Salut et Fraternité
Naples Le 12 Germinal. 7. Louis Du Cros

Mon add. est chez Heigglein n. nég. d'Yverdun artiste Suisse

CATALOGUE

Des Vues de Rome et des environs peintes, à l'acquarelle chez LOUIS DU CROS peintre de Paysage ruë de la croix à Rome.

1 Vue du Pont Mole à Sequins . . . 5	39 Vue générale d'Athène . . . 10
2 Vue du Pont S. Ange avec la girandolle . . . 5	40 Vue générale de l'Amphitéatre de Pola en Istrie . . . 10
3 Vue du Pont rompu . . . 5	
4 Vue du Capitole à l'éffet du jour . . . 5	Le 40 Vues cy dessus peintes en Miniature dans le plus petit format en 24. se vendent 12 Paules la Piéce et 43 Ecus toute la Collection.
5 Vu du Capitole à l'éffet de nuit . . . 5	
6 Vue de la Roche Tarpeienne . . . 5	
7 Vue Générale du Forum Romanum	
8 Vue du Temple de Jupiter tonnant . . . 5	
9 Vue du Temple de la Concorde	*Suite de douze vue moiennes à Sequins 2 ½*
10 Vue du Temple d'Antonin et Faustine	
11 Vue du Temple de Jupiter Stator . . . 5	1 Vue du Tombeau d'Adrien ou château S. Ange . 2 ½
12 Vue du Temple de la paix . . . 5	2 Vue des Thermes de Tite . . . 2 ½
13 Vue du Temple de Minerva Medica . . . 5	3 Vue du Temple de Minerve du forum de Nerva 2 ½
14 Vue de l'Arc de Tite Vespasien . . . 5	4 Vue de l'Arc de Constantin . . . 2 ½
15 Vue laterale de l'Arc de Septime Severe . . . 5	5 Vue de la Piramide de Cajus Cestius . . . 2 ½
16 Vue générale du Colisé externe . . . 5	6 Vue de la Colonne Antonine . . . 2 ½
17 Vue de l'interieur du dit . . . 5	7 Vue de la Colonne Trajane . . . 2 ½
18 Vue des Thermes de Diocletien . . . 5	8 Vue du Temple de Pestum . . . 2 ½
19 Vue des Thermes de Caracalla . . . 5	9 Vue de l'interieur du dit Temple à deux ordres d'Architecture . . . 2 ½
20 Vue de l'interieur des dits . . . 5	10 Vue du même Temple de Pestum . . . 2 ½
21 Vue de l'exterieur du Pantheon . . . 5	11 Vue du Gimnasium de Pestum . . . 2 ½
22 Vue de l'illumination dans le Pantheon à l'exposition des 40. heures . . . 5	
23 Vue de l'illumination de la Croix à l'Eglise de S. Pierre . . . 5	*Suite de douze petites Vues.*
24 Vue du Temple de Minerve du forum Nerva . 5	
25 Vue du Pont Lugano, et du Sepulchre de la famille Plautius . . . 5	1 Vue de la Cascade de Tivoli . . . Sequin 1
26 Vue du Pont Salara sul re Teverone . . . 5	2 Vue de la Cascade de Terni . . . 1
27 Vue du Temple de la Sibille . . . 5	3 Vue de la Grotte de Neptune . . . 1
28 Vue de la grotte de Neptune . . . 5	4 Vue de la Grotte de Palazzola . . . 1
29 Vue generale des Cascatelles de Tivoli . . . 5	5 Vue de la Riccia . . . 1
30 Vue de l'exterieur des Ecuries de Mecene à Tivoli . . . 5	6 Vue des Marets Pontains . . . 1
31 Vue de l'interieur des dits . . . 5	7 Vue de la Porte de la Ville Adrienne . . . 1
32 Vue du Pont d'Auguste à Narni . . . 5	8 Vue des Tombeaux des Horaces et Curiaces . 1
33 Vue générale de la Cascade de Terni . . . 5	9 Vue du Lac de Nemy . . . 1
34 Vue en face de la ditte Cascade . . . 5	10 Vue du Lac d'Albane . . . 1
35 Vue du Lac de Trasiméne . . . 5	11 Vue du Lac de Bolsene . . . 1
36 Grande vue generale de S. Pierre de la Place et des environs au moment de la Benediction . . . Seq. 10	12 Vue du Lac de Trasimene . . . 1
	Vues du Golfe de Naples à Sequins 2 ½
37 Vue de l'interieur de l'Eglise de S. Pierre 10	1 Vue du Temple de Jupiter Serapis à Pouzzol . 2 ½
38 Vue générale de Rome . . . 10	2 Vue du Golfe de Baye et des Etudes de Neron . 2 ½
	3 Vue du Golfe de Pouzzol, et de l'isle d'Ischia . 2 ½
	4 Vue du Pont de Caligola ou Mole de Pouzzol . 2 ½
	5 Deux grandes Vues de la Ville de Naple . Seq. 5

CATALOGUE
DES VUES DE LA SICILE

Celles des Monumens antiques , comme Temples Theatres , Amphitheatres , Tombeaux , Vües générales des Villes , des Cités pittorèsque ou historiques, Volcans etc. Le grand nombre d' Amateurs , qui desirent connoitre cette Isle celebre , et celle de Malthe , vient d' engager Louis Du Cros Peintre de Paysage a Rome de donner au Public par souscription les 24. Vües suivantes sur grand papier de Hollande à 5. Sequins chaque piéce.

1 Vue générale de Palerme prise du Montreal .
2 Vue du Théatre de Taurominum et de l' Etna .
3 Vue du Temple de la Concorde de Girgenti .
4 Vue laterale du Temple de Junon Lucinia .
5 Vue du Temple de Junon en premier plan , et celui de la Concorde en Second.
6 Vue de l'intérieur du Temple de la Concorde à Girgenti.
7 Vue du Sepulcre de Theron à Girgenti .
8 Vue du Temple d' Heroule à Girgenti.
9 Vue du Temple de Vulcain à Girgenti ·
10 Vue de celui d' Esculape .
11 Vue du Temple de Jupiter Olympien .
12 Vue de la Ville de Girgenti ou Agrigentum moderne .
13 Vue de la Fontaine d' Arethuse à Syracuse .
14 Vue de l' Oreille de Denis à Syracuse .

15 Vue de l'Amphitheatre de Syracuse .
16 Vue de la Palazzata de Messine .
17 Vue de l'intérieur de la Ville de Messine ruinée par le Tremblement de terre de l'an 1784. 7. Sequins
18 Vue générale du temple de Sogeste .
19 Vue Laterale du Temple de Segeste .
20 Vue de la Ville de Catagne et de l' Etna .
21 Vue de la Fouille de l'Amphirheatre à Catagne .
22 Vue du Temple de Jupiter a Selinonte .
23 Vue de la Valette ou Cité Triomphante à Malthe a 7.Seq.
24 Vue du Port-aux Galéres , et de l'Arsenal à Malthe .

Pour rendre cet Ouvrage plus intéressant et plus instructif , le susdit Editeur se propose de publier une Description succinte mais suffisante pour donner à connoitre à Messieurs les Amateurs la partie historique de cette Isle ; l'epoque et la cause qui a coopéré à faire batir tel ou tel monument ; telle de sa ruine ; quelques legeres remarques sur son Architecture et sur les Pays d'alentour : cela évitera à Messieurs les Souscripteurs les penibles recherches qui ne peuvent se faire que sur les lieux , sans oter aux savans la liberté de connoitre à fond tout ce qui , dans une brochure n' est qu' exposé.

APPENDIX 3

**Note on conservation, pasted by Ducros onto the
back of his pictures.**
Lausanne (MCBA)

AVIS

Il est nécessaire pour la conservation des Tableaux en général , de les soustraire aux injures de l'air et de la poussiére . Les précautions qu'il faut prendre pour les Sujets peints à l'acquarelle sont .

1. De ne pas les exposer au Soleil , à un trop grand jour et à l'humidité .

2. De les tenir sous glace embordurée , ayant soin de faire coller une légére bande de papier intérieurement de la bordure qui prenne deux lignes sur la glace et deux lignes sur le battant de la bordure ; de metre une planche derriére le dessin , et d'y coller également du papier pour empêcher l'air et les insectes d'y entrer . On peut tenir devant le Tableau un rideau de Taffetas que l'on tire pour voir ; à l'aide de cette précaution, l'aquarelle se conserve toujours dans toute sa beauté

Remede contre les Gerses .

3. On préserve la colle d'Amidon des Gerses en y joignant une poudre extrêmement fine composée de Colloquinte , de Poivre rouge et d'Euphorbe

4. La derniére précaution est de passer une couche de Vernis fait avec de la Cire et de l'huile , sur toutes les bandes de papier collées pour defendre l'emtrée aux insectes . Avec ces precautions on est assuré de la parfaite conservation des Tableaux .

106

APPENDIX 4

Map of Switzerland and Italy showing the principal places where Ducros painted.
(Designed by Inès Lamunière and Patrick Devanthéry).

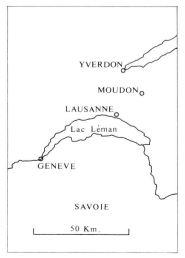

APPENDIX 5

Nuova Pianta di Roma, 1748
by Giovanni Battista Nolli
(detail, The British Library Board)

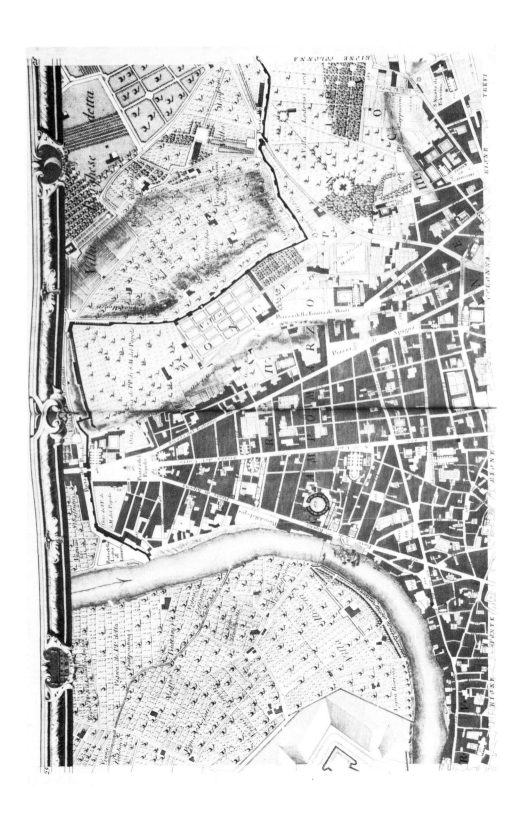

TOPOGRAPHICAL INDEX

Numbers refer to catalogue entries

PHOTOGRAPHIC ACKNOWLEDGEMENTS

We wish to thank the following for permission to reproduce works in their collections:

Amsterdam, Rijksprentenkabinet: cat 51–53: fig 2

Berlin, Verwaltung der Staatlichen Schlösser und Gärten: fig 8, 9, 10

Bern, Kunstmuseum: fig 3, 4

Frankfurt am Main, Freies Deutsches Hochstift-Frankfurter Goethe-Museum: cat 54

Lausanne, Musée Cantonal des Beaux-Arts (J. Cl. Ducret photograph): colour plates I–XII; cat 1–50; fig 1, 5; fig A, L; Appendix 3

Lausanne, Bibliothèque cantonale et Université (Delessert photograph): fig E

London, The Board of the British Library: cat 82; fig 14

London, Trustees of the British Museum: cat 65–67

London, Courtauld Institute of Art: fig D

London, Trustees of the Victoria and Albert Museum: cat 76, fig C

Manchester, The Whitworth Art Gallery, University of Manchester: cat 63–64

Milan, Civica Raccolta delle stampe Achille Bertarelli: fig O

Munich, Bayerische Staatsbibliothek: cat 57–62

Naples, Soprintendenza per i Beni Artistici e Storici: fig G

The National Trust, Dunham Massey: cat 74; fig Q

The National Trust, Stourhead: cat 68–73, 80; Appendix 1

Paris, Bibliothèque Nationale: fig H

Paris, Ministère des Affaires Etrangères: Appendix 2

Pavlovsk, Palace and Museum: cat 56; fig M, P

Private Collections: cat 75, 77–79

Rome, Biblioteca Statale Angelica; fig F, I

Rome, Museo di Roma (Oscar Savio fotografo): cat 55

Rome, Istituto Nazionale per la Grafica: fig 11; fig N

Zürich, Boissonnas SA et W. P. Prescott; fig 12, 13; fig K

Zürich, Kupferstichkabinet der ETH; fig 6

Zürich, The Swiss Institute for Art Research; fig B